This volume's authors bring to life a constructivist approach to addressing challenging behavior that is inclusive, reflective, and collaborative. Their proactive orientation speaks to the classroom environment, teaching practices, curriculum approaches, specialized strategies, and all-important partnerships with families. Through the book's scenarios and invitations for reflection, early childhood educators will gain insights and practical guidance for using strategies that support all children's learning.

—**Janet Thompson**, *Director, Early Childhood Lab School, University of California, Davis*

Gayle Mindes and her colleagues have provided an impressive and much needed service to the early childhood profession with the publication of *Teaching Children with Challenging Behaviors*. They have crafted an engaging, comprehensive, practical, and applied approach to guiding the behaviors of difficult-to-manage children. Professionals in all early childhood settings will benefit from their wise counsel and sound advice. As a result, they have earned the profession's gratitude and thanks.

—**George S. Morrison, Ed.D**, *Emeritus Professor of Early Childhood Education, The University of North Texas*

Teaching Children with Challenging Behaviors

Teaching Children with Challenging Behaviors provides early childhood educators with a guide to developmentally appropriate practice for working with children who exhibit challenging behaviors, as well as perspectives for experienced teachers to reflect upon best practices in today's complex world. This highly practical book addresses systemic issues such as classroom management techniques; social, emotional, and behavioral support strategies; curriculum, assessment, and utilization of technology; and bridging the existing gap between mental health providers, families, and early childhood professionals. Written in nontechnical language with support from current research, this book will help you navigate the sometimes treacherous terrain of teaching children with challenging behaviors.

Gayle Mindes is Professor of Education at DePaul University, Chicago, United States.

**Other Eye On Education Books
Available from Routledge**
(www.routledge.com/eyeoneducation)

**Better Lesson Plans, Better Lessons:
Practical Strategies for Planning from Standards**
Ben Curran

**Your First Year:
How to Survive and Thrive as a New Teacher**
Todd Whitaker, Madeline Whitaker, and Katherine Whitaker

Dealing With Difficult Parents, 2nd Edition
Todd Whitaker and Douglas J. Fiore

**Get Organized!
Time Management for School Leaders, 2nd Edition**
Frank Buck

Leading Schools in an Era of Declining Resources
J. Howard Johnston and Ronald Williamson

**Creating a Classroom Culture That Supports the Common Core:
Teaching Questioning, Conversation Techniques,
and Other Essential Skills**
Brian Harris

Teaching Children with Challenging Behaviors

Practical Strategies for Early Childhood Educators

Edited by
Gayle Mindes

NEW YORK AND LONDON

First published 2018
by Routledge
711 Third Avenue, New York, NY 10017

and by Routledge
2 Park Square, Milton Park, Abingdon, Oxon, OX14 4RN

Routledge is an imprint of the Taylor & Francis Group, an informa business

© 2018 Taylor & Francis

The right of Gayle Mindes to be identified as the author of the editorial material, and of the authors for their individual chapters, has been asserted in accordance with sections 77 and 78 of the Copyright, Designs and Patents Act 1988.

All rights reserved. No part of this book may be reprinted or reproduced or utilised in any form or by any electronic, mechanical, or other means, now known or hereafter invented, including photocopying and recording, or in any information storage or retrieval system, without permission in writing from the publishers.

Trademark notice: Product or corporate names may be trademarks or registered trademarks, and are used only for identification and explanation without intent to infringe.

Library of Congress Cataloging-in-Publication Data
A catalog record for this book has been requested

ISBN: 978-1-138-93620-1 (hbk)
ISBN: 978-1-138-93622-5 (pbk)
ISBN: 978-1-315-67697-5 (ebk)

Typeset in Palatino
by Apex CoVantage, LLC

To friends, colleagues, and family who encouraged
this work and made it happen.

Gayle

Contents

Preface xiii
Editor's Acknowledgments xvi
Meet the Authors xvii

1 Supporting Behavior and Learning for All Young Children 1
Gayle Mindes

Teaching Young Children in Classrooms 1
    Teachers in Charge 2
    Exclusion from Activities and Expulsion 3
    Cost to Children, Families, and Teachers 3
    Teachers Must Produce Outcomes 4
    Teachers Quit 4
    Social Competence 5
    Examples of Externalized Challenging Behaviors 6
    Teachers Act Immediately 7
Dealing with Challenging Behavior 8
    Merely Annoying Behaviors 9
Why Manage Challenging Behavior? 11
    Safety and Security 11
    Socializing Children for School 11
    Teachers' Contributions to Self-Empowered Learners .. 13
    Teaching as an Emotional Experience 14
    Knowing Yourself to Be an Effective Teacher 14
    Including Everyone and Providing for All 16
    English Learners 17
    Children with Difficult Family Situations 17
Prevention Works 19
Conclusion 19
Chapter 1 Activities 19
    Activity 1 19
    Activity 2 20
    Activity 3 20

2 Setting the Stage for Success 22
Kathleen M. Sheridan

Classroom Environment......................................22
    Classroom Space and Physical Environment 25
    Setting Up Learning Centers..............................27
    Classroom Materials.....................................28
    Classroom Surfaces and Displays.........................32
Personal Interactions 32
    Conflict Resolution 41
    Morning Meetings.......................................46
    Class Meetings...46
Rules and Rituals in School 48
Routines and Schedules 51
Developmentally Appropriate Guidance 53
    Executive Function 55
    PBIS and Bullying 57
Successful Teaching...58
    Cultural Relevance 59
Summing It Up 61
Chapter 2 Activities..62
    Activity 1 62
    Activity 2 62
    Activity 3 63

3 Implementing Effective Curriculum 64
Dom Gullo

Implementing Developmental Appropriate Practice...........64
    Connections Between Curriculum and Strategies 65
    Universal Design for Learning 68
    Differentiated Instruction................................69
    Summary 71
Constructivist Early Childhood Curriculum 72
    Teaching and Learning from a Constructivist Approach 73
    Project Approach.......................................78
    Linking Curriculum to Required Outcomes................82
Curriculum and External State Standards.....................84
Academic Language 86
Social-Emotional Learning...................................87
The Dimensions of Assessment..............................90

Conclusions 92
  Chapter 3 Activities. 93
     Activity 1 93
     Activity 2 93
     Activity 3 94
     Activity 4 94
     Activity 5 95

4 **Classroom Management with Special Techniques for Managing Challenging Behaviors** 96
  Bridget Amory

  Creating a Positive Learning Environment. 97
  Managing the Early Childhood Classroom. 101
  Strategies for Organizing the Physical Environment. 102
  Establishing Procedures and Routines. 105
  Prevention and Strategies to Stay Ahead of Behaviors 107
     Consistency 108
     Supporting Individuals 108
  Dealing with Disruption 109
  Power Struggles. 110
  Special Interventions. 113
     Scenario 1 116
     Scenario 2 117
  Special Cues. 118
     Positive Reinforcement. 119
     Social Stories 120
     Video Recording and Discussion 121
  Professional Reflections 122
  Summary 123
  Chapter 4 Activities. 124
     Jonas Smith. 124
     Suzy Trumble. 126
     Phillip Turner. 127

5 **Collaborating for Success** 129
  Megan Schumaker-Murphy

  Why Should I Concern Myself with Relationships
     with Young Children's Families? 129
  Understanding Modern Families 131

Strategies for Building and Maintaining Successful
    Relationships 137
    Become Culturally Competent 137
    Build Relationships Before a Problem Occurs 144
    Problem-solve Together 150
    Involve Families in Scheduling Meetings and
        School Events. 151
    Report Successes More Often Than Failures
        and Give It Time 152
Communicating Difficult News or Major Concerns 153
Challenging Families 157
Remember That You and the Family Are on the Same Team . . . 158
Chapter 5 Activities. 159
    Activity 1 159
    Activity 2 159
    Activity 3 160

Appendix 161
    Terms to Know. 161
    Study Questions 162
    For Additional Information. 164
    Additional Online Resources 166
    DEC Position Statement on Challenging Behavior 167
    Standing Together Against Suspension &
        Expulsion in Early Childhood. 169
References. 171

Preface

Teachers who want to serve in early childhood settings frequently say that they "love little kids." They are drawn to the energy, spontaneity, sometimes silly behavior, and the delightful things children do and say. Teachers of young children value creativity, the play of young children, and collaborating with families. Early childhood teachers want to see their charges learn and develop increasing skills and competencies. But teaching today involves many opportunities and challenges across the various early childhood settings. Children come to child care at younger ages and from increasingly culturally diverse backgrounds. As well, we have come to value the importance of teaching young children in inclusive environments—that is, including children with disabilities. Thus, the early childhood teacher's role grows increasingly complex. One of the most challenging roles for teachers today is the requirement to manage behavior in all of its permutations, including behavior characterized as challenging.

Thinking about challenging behavior on a continuum is complicated in our day and across different conditions throughout the country. The vision for this book is to create a reflective piece on the whole classroom. How do you plan for all the children in your care? Where do you start? What is your role in supporting the development of young children's social and emotional development? All of these are questions that early childhood educators prepare for as they teach in a socioeconomic climate that demands performance from children and accountability from teachers.

To make this book happen, four experts were recruited to write chapters that elucidate developmentally appropriate practice for all children. That is, as early childhood teachers, what must we think about to be sure that we support young children's development of social competency, beginning from wherever they are when they enter the classroom? Flowing from this reflection, what are necessary modifications for children who require more assistance to function effectively in a classroom? How do we as teachers provide social and emotional cues so that each child can learn? How do we preserve order? These overall questions are explored in each of the following chapters:

- Chapter 1, "Supporting Behavior and Learning for All Young Children," presents an overview of our responsibilities as teachers to promote learning, mentor young children's social-emotional skill development, and to maintain order for the health and safety of all in our care.
- Chapter 2, "Setting the Stage for Success," describes all of the attributes of a setting designed for effective learning. All aspects of the classroom environment from the physical to the routines, rules, and Positive Behavioral Intervention and Supports (PBIS) are delineated.
- Chapter 3, "Implementing Effective Curriculum," shows ways to implement the various standards and curricular expectations through intentional teaching in ways that document achievement and individualized instruction.
- Chapter 4, "Classroom Management with Special Techniques for Managing Challenging Behaviors," features ways to organize for order in the social realm of the classroom, as well as functional behavioral analysis and other specialized approaches to support children with challenging behavior.
- Chapter 5, "Collaborating for Success," includes ways to structure relationships with families in the usual situations and in those where children are expressing challenging behavior. Collaborating with families is an essential feature of our work as early childhood educators.

About This Book

This book is written for the teacher who wants to understand the broad range of issues associated with providing exciting educational experiences for all young children, including those who present behavior that is challenging. Accordingly, the book reflects the knowledge base of early childhood education, early childhood special education, and culturally responsive teaching. It provides illustrations of developmentally appropriate practice for prospective teachers, as well as perspectives for experienced teachers to reflect upon best practices in today's complex world. The book approaches managing challenging behavior as an integral part of the teaching and learning process. Key components of the setting, the curriculum, the management system, and family collaboration are illustrated. The book is written in non-technical language with support from current research.

Organization of the Book

The book is organized holistically. Chapter 1 orients the reader to the saliency of the issues surrounding preparation for children presenting challenging behavior. Chapter 2 highlights the setting of the class space and community. Chapter 3 underlines the importance of developmentally appropriate curriculum in supporting learners who present challenging behavior. Chapter 4 tackles issues around structuring the management of early childhood settings to include special techniques for child behavior that is challenging. Chapter 5 provides a framework for collaborating with families to support all learners and especially those whose children are presenting challenging behavior.

Editor's Acknowledgments

Thank you to the thousands of children, families, teacher candidates, and colleagues who have influenced my thinking over the years. Special thanks to George S. Morrison, Professor of Education at the University of North Texas, who guided my developmental thinking about this book project and offered critical reviews of the work in progress. Thanks to Janet Thompson, Director of Early Childhood Laboratory (ECL), Center for Child and Family Studies at the University of California, Davis, and Ross A. Thompson, Director of the Social Emotional Development Lab, for their contributions to the initial prospectus for this project. Thanks to Elizabeth H. White, educational consultant, and to Kathleen M. Sheridan, who critically read early versions of various chapters. Thanks to Rafik Antar, graduate assistant extraordinaire, who contributed thoughtful comments and technical expertise to the production of the manuscript, as well as writing the section on functional behavioral assessment in Chapter 5. Thanks to Jonathan Mindes who provided developmental editing throughout the process. And thanks especially to the authors of the chapters—Bridget Amory, Dom Gullo, Megan Schumaker-Murphy, and Kathleen M. Sheridan—who provided expertise and valuable anecdotes to make the book live and sing.

We all appreciate the support, encouragement, and vision of Alex Masulis, Senior Editor, Lauren Franklin, Editorial Assistant, and others behind the scenes at Routledge.

—Gayle Mindes, 2017

Meet the Authors

Bridget Amory, EdD serves as the Director of Elementary Education in the Milford School District, where she works with a dynamic team of professionals who work to educate a diverse population of learners. She additionally works as an adjunct instructor at Wilmington University helping to develop curriculum and prepare preservice educators. She is an experienced early childhood educator and administrator who is passionate about working collaboratively to improve educational outcomes for children and families and is grateful to have a career where she continues to be challenged.

Dominic F. Gullo, PhD is a Professor of Early Childhood Education and the Associate Dean for Research in the School of Education at Drexel University in Philadelphia. His specializations in early childhood education are in urban education, children of poverty, assessment and evaluation, curriculum development, and early language and literacy.

Dom is a former member of the Governing Board of the National Association for the Education of Young Children (NAEYC). He is the author of five books, four early childhood curricula, more than 75 peer-reviewed research-based publications, and more than 25 book chapters. His research interests include studying the relative and long-range effects of factors associated with risk and resiliency on children's school readiness, academic performance, and social adaptation to school routine, particularly among urban children who reside in homes of economic poverty.

Dom has completed writing the second edition of his book, *Understanding assessment and evaluation in early childhood education* (Teachers College Press) and is the Editor of the NAEYC publication *K-Today: teaching and learning in the kindergarten year*. He has presented his work both nationally and internationally. He consults extensively with school districts locally, nationally, and internationally on early childhood issues related to assessment, developmentally appropriate practice, and child development.

Gayle Mindes, EdD is Professor of Education at DePaul University in Chicago. She teaches in the preservice early childhood and doctoral programs there. Gayle, a life-long urban educator, writes and speaks on the topics of assessment, social studies, and kindergarten. Her recent books include Mindes, G., and Jung, L. A., (2015) *Assessing young children, 5th ed*. Upper Saddle River, NJ: Pearson; and *Social studies for young children: Preschool and primary curriculum anchor*, (2014) 2nd edition. Lanham, MD: Rowman & Littlefield Publishers, Inc. She is a consulting editor for NAEYC, and served as co-editor with Derry Koralek for Pushing up social studies from early childhood to the world. *Young Children*. July 2015. Mindes regularly presents at NAEYC conferences and has publications on kindergarten published by the association.

Megan Schumaker-Murphy has served more than 300 families with young children as a special education teacher, early interventionist, and teacher educator. She has a master's degree in early childhood special education from the University of Illinois at Chicago. Megan is a doctoral student and part-time faculty member at DePaul University. A practitioner at heart, Megan's research interests focus on understanding and improving the lives of families with children with disabilities and integrating best practice into service provision. She lives in Chicago with her family, where she maintains a small early intervention practice.

Kathleen M. Sheridan, PhD is an Associate Professor in the Educational Psychology Department in the College of Education at the University of Illinois at Chicago. In addition, she is a visiting scholar at the Institute for Government and Public Affairs at the University of Illinois. She received her doctorate in Child and Family Studies from the University of Wisconsin–Madison and her masters from Washington University in St Louis. Kathy regularly presents and publishes on a variety of topics related to education and is the lead Principal Investigator on the Early Math Matters: Math at Home CME Group Foundation grant-funded project at the University of Illinois at Chicago.

1

Supporting Behavior and Learning for All Young Children

Gayle Mindes

In this chapter, we will look at classroom life, define challenging behavior, and discuss teacher responsibilities for the early childhood classrooms of today. The discussion emphasizes the critical role that teachers play in meeting learning outcomes, developing social competence in individual children, and maintaining a safe, secure environment for all children to learn and thrive. A definition of challenging behavior begins the chapter. Included topics are the high rate of expulsion of children from early childhood settings and the essential role for teachers in promoting self-empowerment of all learners.

Teaching Young Children in Classrooms

Children come to our classrooms with various social and emotional skills that manifest themselves in their behavior. As teachers, we are charged with facilitating behaviors that will lead to enhanced social competence with both individual behavioral skills and the capacity to function effectively in a community of learners. Classrooms are inherently social structures of relationships between teachers and individual children and among children. The way the social structure of the classroom plays out is influenced by children's experiences in group settings and their cultural and family backgrounds. In addition, the social relationships are influenced by personal views of appropriate child behavior and the teacher's confidence in their role. All of the social aspects occur within a philosophical orientation to program and curriculum wherein learning academics must occur.

Teachers in Charge

In the arena of social relationships and the school or child care center's program goals and philosophy, the one immutable requirement is that the teacher must be in charge of the room—keeping order and safety firmly in mind. Thus, what vexes teachers the most is behavior that interferes in the work of the classroom—the learning for all young children. In this book, we will explore ways to deal with behavior that is difficult to manage, including the extremes of difficult behavior known as *externalized challenging behavior*.

> Challenging behavior that is externalized is a child's outburst and loss of self-control. For example, hitting others, kicking,

FIGURE 1.1 Teacher leading a class discussion.
Source: iStock

screaming, and spitting are very challenging to handle in the classroom. The child exhibiting such behavior demands teacher attention—first so the child can be protected from potentially hurting self or others, and second to reassure the child who is behaving this way that the child's perceived "threat" will stop.

Extreme behavior is also frightening for other children in the classroom and difficult to manage. Unfortunately, too often many teachers are not successful in managing this difficult behavior—and often the solution is to remove the child from the situation.

Exclusion from Activities and Expulsion

When teachers are unable to manage children's behavior, they often send children to a corner of the room, have an assistant remove the child who is out of control, and finally build a case for suspension and expulsion from the program. The statistics for expulsion from early childhood state-funded programs are three times higher than for K–12 schools. In 2008, there were 6.7 expulsions for every 1,000 preschoolers in these programs. The highest number of children were the ones at the older end of the continuum and African American boys. The numbers of young children expelled from private child care centers are even higher (Gilliam, 2008). We cannot continue to function in the best interest of young children by operating from an exclusion perspective. Young children and their families count on continuity of learning experiences for optimum child development.

Cost to Children, Families, and Teachers

The cost to children, families, and teachers for excluding children from child care settings is not simply a financial burden for families; it is most of all an emotional one. Families must deal with searching for a new child care arrangement, potential disruption of their own work schedule, comforting their children, and handling feelings of failure. All of these responses and necessary actions tax the family structure and affect a child's ultimate successful learning in school. A joint policy statement by the US Department of Education and the US Department of Health and Human Services (2014) calls for early childhood educators to prevent and severely limit the suspension and expulsion of children from early childhood settings. Statistics from these agencies and others reveal that not only are young children suspended and excluded at higher rates than older elementary and high schoolers, but also the actions show racial and gender bias. In addition to the US Department of Education and US Department of Health and Human Services policy statement, the National Association for the Education for Young Children created the advocacy action statement: *Standing together against suspension and expulsion in early childhood* (2016), which highlights statistics, research, and action items related to teacher development and program sensitivity for all children. While being sensitive to children's individual needs for social-emotional development, teachers today must meet program outcome requirements that may at times seem incongruent with attention to facilitation of children's social and emotional skills.

Teachers Must Produce Outcomes

For teachers, the pressure to create the conditions for child success at any age is enormous. Teachers must balance the needs of individuals with the needs of the group. They must scaffold individual children to be effective learners and community members, while keeping potential chaos at bay. Teacher decisions must also be made at lightning speed. They must constantly ask themselves questions such as, what behavior can be ignored momentarily? Will the group tolerate Arthur's hysterical crying for a few minutes while we are cleaning up? Can I verbally reassure Arthur from across the room? Will everyone burst into tears? Will they make fun of Arthur? Will a classmate go to Arthur's aid? All of these possible scenarios will be affected by the teacher's relationship with the group, each individual, the routines established, the ages of the children involved, and many other factors. For teachers, who must make these split-second intervene or don't intervene decisions, on a daily basis, the balance of "smooth functioning" versus chaos determines whether learning occurs and whether teachers feel successful in meeting the requirements of the curriculum and the children they serve. If there is an imbalance in teachers' perceptions of their capacities to organize, teach, nurture, and "manage the classroom" while coping with behavior that is challenging, there is the risk that highly qualified teachers hoping to make a difference in the lives of children will give up and leave the field.

Teachers Quit

The *2005 Spotlight: Mobility in the teacher workforce* (2014) shows that one of the five most common reasons for leaving the field is problematic student behavior. One manifestation of teacher dissatisfaction is frustration and anger that may occur when a particular child cannot meet academic demands (Chang, 2009 in McCarthy, Lineback, & Reiser, 2014). The frustration and anger occurs based on the teacher's perception of the situation. Thus, if the teacher sees that a child is messing around when a group lesson is being presented, they might perceive that the child is interfering with the learning goal for that time period and creating a group distraction. The feelings of frustration may be exacerbated when teachers cope by employing yelling, humiliation of children, group punishment, and showing negative attitudes toward individual students.

To combat feelings of frustration and anger toward children, teachers must have a number of tools, a great deal of knowledge about child behavior, and the capacity to reflect upon their practices. If teachers feel self-confident in their capacity to instruct, individualize, and to collaborate with children in advancing learning, they can be effective with children and secure in their effectiveness in managing the instruction and the child behavior. In this book, we will focus on the elements of setting the stage for learning success through the lens of putting behavior first, since it is disruptive behavior that saps teacher confidence and contributes to the reasons teachers opt out of the profession. In this way, we contribute to the development of each child's social-emotional learning and self-efficacy as a learner in a social setting, and ultimately facilitate social competence.

Social Competence

For our purposes, then, what should we be thinking about regarding child behavior in the classroom? If we seek to create a productive learning environment, then we must both promote **social competence**, which is, broadly speaking, the ability of young children to get along with others. In the classroom, social competence is complicated with the requirement that each child must conform to the structure of the classroom, as well as interact with others who may not share the same cultural values and experiences.

Besides fostering social competence for children who have varying experiences in group situations and who are learning the ropes of school, teachers have to manage behavioral outbursts on a continuum from the merely annoying to those that are outright dangerous. These are not always easily solvable, but here we will discuss some ways of tackling the complexity of managing the classroom.

The following scenarios depict some of the situations teachers might face on a daily basis.

Examples of Externalized Challenging Behaviors

Three-year-old Alessandra does not speak in her Head Start class, and she is not interested in any of the activities available during free play. She wanders the room with her hand outstretched, approaching her friends to pat them on the cheek or to scratch them. Neither the teacher nor the children know which action to expect. Alessandra's behavior is unpredictable and thus challenging for both the children and the teacher: The children never know whether they will be hurt and the teacher is unsure what this behavior means to Alessandra. The children exclude her from their play and the teacher can't always be by her side. What to do?

Harold, a 4-year-old in a child care center, rarely stops moving during his eight-hour day there. He shouts out when one of the two teachers reads a story to the group in the circle, knocks over his friends' block structures, and runs out of the room. The teachers fret, because they are worried that they may not immediately see him running away—thus putting Harold in danger. Martha and Howard, Harold's parents, are mystified about the teachers' reports. They claim he is fine at home, although they are worried that he doesn't get invitations to birthday parties and rarely gets requests to play at classmates' homes.

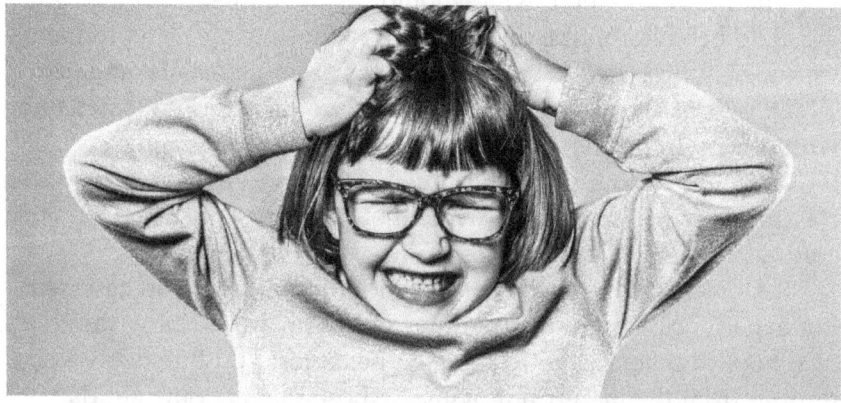

FIGURE 1.2 Example of an angry child.
Source: iStock

How can Harold's parents and his teacher help him when they have totally different perceptions about his behaviors in school?

First graders complain to Ms. Hawthorne that someone is pinching them and she can see bruises on their arms. The complaint often comes when the children are standing in line to go to recess or to specials. After several days of watching Lurleen and quizzing the children, she discovers that Lurleen is the culprit. In front of the children, she pulls Lurleen out of line and tells her in a firm voice: "You can't pinch your friends. It hurts them. I am going to call your family, right after school. They will have to come to a conference with me." The next day, Lurleen arrives at school, as usual, but she refuses to talk. She will not answer Ms. Hawthorne's questions, read aloud, or talk to classmates in the classroom, although children report that she talks to them on the playground. This behavior continues for several weeks. A student teacher, Ms. Bell arrives; Ms. Hawthorne asks Ms. Bell to pretend that she doesn't know that Lurleen is mute during class. As soon as Ms. Bell asks Lurleen to read, the other children in the group say: "She doesn't talk." How can Ms. Hawthorn help Lurleen? What resources does she have available to her in the school setting to assist her in assessing the situation?

In each of these scenarios, children are using behavior to express themselves. Sometimes it is immediately apparent as to why the behavior occurs; sometimes we may need to look more closely at the context and the behavior to figure out what is going on. Nevertheless, faced with these situations, each teacher must deal with the behavior expeditiously so that learning can occur for everyone.

Teachers Act Immediately

In each of these scenarios, teachers face child behavior that disrupts the class community. These are serious behaviors challenging the teacher to act quickly and responsively, so that the children exhibiting outbursts can learn the social skills necessary for classroom success and gain emotional security. Some of the behaviors are dangerous to the life of the classroom, as well as to the children in the setting. In other situations, teachers may see behaviors requiring immediate action, but the disruptions may be merely annoying, such as Sarah's flicking of the lights on and off in the classroom during cleanup time. Always, teachers worry about contagion. They may worry whether other children "catch" the "bad" habits or whether there will be a revolt.

No one will feel secure and safe when there is the possibility that the 3-year-olds are in charge, when children feel frightened of being hurt, or of losing their possessions, or having their toys broken. But most of all, teachers need to feel secure. They must be in charge, in control, effective in their relationships and in facilitating learning. Thus, as a teacher, you must learn how to manage the complexities of creating, maintaining, and individualizing an effective learning environment. In this way, you assure all the children in your care that they can be self-empowered learners.

Dealing with Challenging Behavior

In a classroom set up for learning, the adult (i.e., the teacher) must be in control of self and react with empathy, authority, and reassurance toward each individual child. Then, there is the rest of the class. The teacher must help the other children to feel safe, comfortable, and reassured that all will be calm in the classroom. In this way, children control their own behavior and children thrive in the learning community. While child behavior is the focus of this book and challenging behavior becomes center stage in any classroom, teachers are primarily accountable for meeting curricular outcomes. So, how do teachers do both—manage behavior and create a learning community for everyone? First, teachers must (and usually do) recognize challenging behavior, those incidents that disrupt the calm, engaging learning activities. Second, teachers must learn to effectively manage challenging behavior for the individual learner and the class as a whole. Teachers accomplish this feat by learning effective ways to identify triggers for individual child outbursts, as well as helping young children to gain increasing skill at self-efficacy in social situations. Then, everyone can be a learner.

As defined at the start of this chapter, externalized challenging behavior is loss of self-control by an individual child that must be dealt with immediately. So, in addition to the preceding anecdotes of children showing challenging behavior, extreme behaviors are those that offer a serious incident, such as throwing a chair at another child or adult; behaviors that are persistent, such as running around the classroom, refusing to sit in a seat, or screaming; or those that are intermittent, occurring occasionally with no apparent pattern, such as bursting into tears. All of these extreme behaviors require specialized intervention techniques or adjustments to the classroom environment.

However, along the continuum of behavior there are other troublesome behaviors that are not so severe. For teachers, this means the behavior of children that interferes with learning and social relationships in the classroom setting.

Merely Annoying Behaviors

Besides the extreme instances of challenging behavior, different teachers will define annoying behavior, attention-seeking behavior, and "off-day" behavior as more or less challenging depending on the social context—playground, story time, center time, transition times, field trip, etc.—and their personal expectations for "good" behavior, rooted in their own cultural, familial, and school experiences. A teacher's own experiences and expectations are influenced by their pedagogical philosophy and professional development, as well. For example, can you tolerate a degree of fidgeting, sitting in a chair on knees, or getting up to take a spin around the room, if in all other ways Paul is attending to the task at hand? What about doodling while listening to a story or a classmate's speech? All of these factors influence the classroom climate, the established structure for the class, and the in-the-moment responses of the teacher to a child's behavior. Thus, beyond the definition of challenging behavior, there is a continuum of behaviors that teachers often find difficult to handle. Let's examine some child behaviors and potential teacher responses in the following scenarios.

As soon as Kevin walks into the room, he asks Ms. Smith, "Are we going to lunch today? What time is lunch?" Although Ms. Smith recognizes that Kevin has a neurological condition that causes verbal perseveration—a repetition of words or phrases repetitively—she personally finds this behavior annoying because it happens every day, several times a day. Depending on whether she can work with 6-year-old Kevin to answer his question calmly or work out a routine solution that can reassure him and prevent a migraine on her part, Kevin's behavior will continue to be annoying and creating the potential for Ms. Smith to become impatient or snarly with Kevin and the other children. Ms. Smith can develop solutions for Kevin, but she may also wish to reflect upon her own values and experiences to determine why this behavior is so annoying to her.

Ms. Garcia is chatting with Mrs. Rodriguez about Carlita's trip to see a visiting aunt and uncle. Oswald bursts through the classroom door and begins tapping Ms. Garcia on the arm. He doesn't say "excuse me" or seem to notice that Ms. Garcia and Mrs. Rodriquez are in the middle of a conversation. Whether Ms. Garcia reprimands Oswald sternly ("Can't you see I am talking, Oswald? You must go to your seat and be quiet.") or calmly accepts the interruption and deflects the situation ("Good morning, Oswald, I can see that you are very excited. What is it that you want to tell me? Can it wait just a minute? Mrs. Rodriquez and I are in the middle of something here. Thank you so much for being patient, Oswald, I'll come right over to your seat to hear your news.") will depend on Ms. Garcia's history with Oswald, her classroom structure, her relationship with families, as well as her perspective on whether children should interrupt adults who are conversing.

Out on the playground, Rebecca starts kicking David; he starts to kick back when Arnold says, "you can't kick girls!" Ms. Foster is standing nearby. She decides to do nothing and lets the children figure out the solution. She believes that adults should wait for children to solve problems, even if it means there is a risk that punches may result. Ms. Foster is influenced by the value she places on child autonomy.

In each of these scenarios and in the countless behavioral incidents that occur throughout the life in the classroom, there are little behaviors that teachers find difficult. The more that you can respect individual differences in child behaviors and accept a bit of twiddling and fidgeting, the fewer conflicts you will have with the class as a whole and with individual children. To help you think about expanding your repertoire of acceptable child behaviors so that learning can occur, we offer here ways to think about your responsibility for being in charge of the classroom that is holistic. The elements considered are as follows:

- classroom environment,
- curriculum,
- classroom management principles, and
- family collaboration.

Consideration of the nuances of each of these elements adds clarity for ensuring child development and learning. We will look at ways to think about challenging behavior on a continuum from the little things that push your personal buttons to the big events presented by children who will require more specific interventions to sustain them in social situations.

Why Manage Challenging Behavior?

Safety and Security
Perhaps the first reason for managing challenging behavior in the classroom is to promote feelings of safety and security for the children within the classroom community. Young children will wonder whether they are safe from potential harm. They may worry: Will David kick me? Will Martha scratch me? Will Wiley spit on me? Can I get away? Will the teacher save me from these assaults? If Karen continues to scream, will the teacher stop her? Why are these kids behaving this way? In the same way, teachers are frustrated and worried that the whole class will "run away" from them. That is, they worry that if a challenge is not "handled," will more children "act out"? Teachers also wonder how to stop the challenging behavior humanely, so that everyone feels safe. In addition, teachers are responsible for educating all of the children. Thus, helping a child with challenging behavior to learn alternative behaviors that are socially accepted in the classroom is part of every teacher's responsibility.

Socializing Children for School
Besides thinking about the safety and security of the children, teachers are aware of their responsibility for helping young children learn the ways schools operate. Teachers are the first to socialize young children in the ways of school. It is here that children learn the cultural norms and values of society (Durkheim, 1973). In the classroom of 2017, we value creating learning environments for all children, where all voices are heard and respected. This kind of community development requires a deep awareness of the cultures of our children and their families, which have shaped the children's early learning experiences.

In Jackson's (1968) portrait of *Life in Classrooms*, which was an analysis of elementary classrooms based on psychological theory and empirical studies, he states that the youngest students learn to deal and may be introduced by the key words: "crowds, praise and power" (p. 10). The key words of *crowds, praise,* and *power* are still important as teachers think about the organization of school, from the preschool years and beyond. Young children are moving from the family system where they may have limited experience with crowds to the child care setting where their needs are not necessarily immediately attended to (e.g., in the one to 10 ratios of child care center). In their own home,

FIGURE 1.3 Children entering class.
Source: iStock

they may have enjoyed an immediate response to their personal needs, and were not necessarily required to share resources, i.e., toys, iPads, family attention. In the family situation, members may have clapped hands, uttered praise, or in other ways rewarded every small achievement. For example, learning to use the bathroom, bouncing a ball, repeating rhymes, and so on may have been skills learned with lavish praise. Or, they may come from homes where they had no one who praised them; they may have experienced a barrage of criticism or big brothers bullying them. Nevertheless, at home, power might be more easily negotiated with siblings rather than with 20 classmates. There would be no need to wait for your turn or wait until the teacher calls on you. At school or in child care settings, young children have early experiences with being judged, by themselves, their teachers, and their peers. Questions such as, who drew the best pumpkin? Who can sit still in the circle? Who can help a peer? are often implied or explicitly stated. Thus, the ways that teachers nurture, empower, and scaffold the community of young scholars paves the way for smooth group interaction and learning. The effective organization of a classroom influences children's attitudes, values, and civic participation. It is in these early years that the foundation for the approach to academics and exploring curiosities is modeled and learned.

Teachers' Contributions to Self-Empowered Learners

When teachers are effective in creating classrooms that are safe, nurturing, and self-empowering for children, children learn valuable interpersonal skills, such as ways to negotiate, build consensus, and strategize to meet learning goals with peers. The teachers' behavior shows children how to negotiate change, cultural diversity, and community responsibility. Teachers show young children how to comfortably relate to strangers and their peers in the social group, especially in preschool, where they have their first experiences with groups of children who must function in some kind of order, such as following the routines and rules necessary for group life. In secure environments, children develop a sense of self-worth, a sense of belonging to a school community, and feelings of trust of teacher, self, and others. They become life-long learners and keen followers of the norms and values of school. All children need experiences in school to support autonomy; foster relationships and interdependence; generate feelings of safety and trust, pleasure and joy; and opportunities for communication (Erikson, 1963; Causton & Tracy-Bronson, 2015).

Thus, teachers in early childhood settings must be sure that their social practices in the classroom foster and generate development of these social-emotional skills. By paying close attention to teaching social skills, and by being aware of ways to intervene with children showing challenging behaviors, teachers contribute to a healthy social-emotional development for their young charges. Children show **social-emotional development** with behaviors demonstrating that they possess the capacity to self-regulate and to interact with peers and adults in social situations. You can see the effects of your interventions that contribute to social-emotional development by observing the ways that children behave in socially appropriate ways, the ways that they control their emotions, and by the growing vocabulary that they use in expressing their wants, needs, and feelings.

Teaching as an Emotional Experience

Teaching is at heart an emotional experience, because each teacher must create a comfortable atmosphere for each of the children to feel safe to risk trying new behaviors and practice new skills. Teachers must model appropriate social interactions and display of their own emotions. "Good teachers are not just well-oiled machines. They are emotional, passionate beings who connect with their students and their work and their classes with pleasure, creativity, challenge and joy" (Hargreaves, 1998, p. 835). Being available emotionally to children and their families requires self-knowledge, for it is your experiences as a child, a family member, and cultural being that influence your beliefs about "appropriate" behavior. Your personal beliefs interact with your curricular approach and shape the tools that you bring as a baseline to the "table" of the classroom. So, to be effective in managing child behavior, you need to have awareness of your own emotional strengths and weaknesses.

Knowing Yourself to Be an Effective Teacher

Factors that contribute to a teacher's effectiveness in this emotional work will be influenced by a teacher's own experiences as a child in their own family and in their school, in addition to the support received from the center or school in solving behavioral conflicts in school. In addition, current stressors in teachers' lives and the outcomes of negative interactions with one or more children may lead to a less-than-calm classroom climate and will influence the teacher emotionally.

"In the heat of conflict, adult cognitions and emotion regulation work in concert to limit, or in some instances enhance, adults' contingent responsiveness and proactive socialization of child self-control and compliance" (Raver, Blair, & Li-Grining, 2012, p. 126).

Increasingly, there is a recognition that the emotional work of teaching includes the capacity to understand our own feelings and to regulate our emotions. We need to understand how our body language and tone of voice influence children in a way that makes the development of social skills accessible to the wide variety of children we teach. Above all, when teaching young children, we want to avoid losing our own self-control by yelling and refusing to consider the child's point of view (Jones, Bouffard, & Weissbourd, 2013, pp. 62–63). This is the work of teaching that contributes to the development of emotional intelligence and social skills in young children. Emotional intelligence is "the ability to perceive emotions and emotional knowledge, and to reflectively regulate emotions so as to promote emotional and intellectual growth" (Mayer & Salovey, 1997, p. 5).

Accordingly, teaching young children requires teachers to consider the development of emotional intelligence as an integral ingredient for the curriculum. Whether or not schools and child care centers pay attention to the development of emotional intelligence with special emotional intelligence programs, it is clear that the work of teaching requires reflection, purposeful observation, and interaction with all young children to promote their social-emotional development and to individualize for children with challenging behavior. Helping children learn nuanced ways to recognize their feelings, and ways to express them appropriately, should be part of the classroom checking in about the way the days are going for the community. This requires being in touch with your own feelings of elation, despair, joy, and excitement, and the capacity to show children ways to be aware and in touch with whether they are mad, frustrated, confused, excited, etc. As early childhood teachers, we serve as modelers and mentors for young children to expand their horizons for appropriate emotional expressive behavior. By the same token, teachers must avoid using faux emotions—that is, false cheerfulness in situations where children are involved in conflict, feeling sad, or behaving "against the rules and routines." Such behavior by teachers diminishes the child's sense of authentic emotional expression and sends mixed messages to children who are learning self-regulation of their own behavior. Finally, of course, we need to assist young children who are unable for a moment in time or on an ongoing basis to control their emotional and social behavior—showing challenging behavior.

Including Everyone and Providing for All

So, the task is complex. We must mentor children for successful participation in society, while delivering content, reaching outcomes, and identifying children who will need more support from our educational system to be successful. But even the best of interventions may require consultation with experts to secure adequate education for all young children. The focus of this book is setting the stage for all young children to be successful in inclusive settings while being aware that consultation for children with externalized challenging behavior is important for the success of their ability to function in the classroom. The child with challenging behavior is but one of those who may have special needs. We must nurture all in our care. As prepared and qualified early childhood teachers, it is important to diminish—not increase—the isolation of young children with special needs who have often been isolated and excluded.

FIGURE 1.4 Children learning.
Source: iStock

As teachers, we are responsible for educating all the children in an inclusive environment. In addition to meeting the learning needs of young children with special needs, our classrooms are increasingly diverse. Therefore, we must provide appropriate learning experiences for children who are learning English and not confuse their issues with language as anything other than frustration with their ability to communicate.

English Learners

We must determine whether behavior that appears challenging is a result of limited understanding of the English language. For children who do not understand the primary language used in the classroom, school may be frightening and the child may show their anxiety through

> acting out, aggression, frustration, anger or resentment; self-directed signs of stress such as refusing to eat, toileting accidents, biting themselves, or pulling their hair; withdrawal, sadness, isolation, depression, or being mute; ignoring directions, being rude or defiant, not listening or participating.
> (Nemeth & Brilliante, 2011, pp. 13–14)

Sensitive teachers will look at the behavior and determine the meaning or goal for the child rather than react out of their own frustration or need to "control" the child and the social situation. In addition, they will study ways to support and encourage children who are English learners as part of their everyday preparation of the learning environment. Our classrooms are diverse, and in addition they include children whose early experiences may be in neglectful or chaotic family structures where the adults need special assistance to provide a stable environment for their children.

Children with Difficult Family Situations

In situations where the whole family needs assistance because of mental health issues or crises of the moment or long term, the children in these families will need our special attention to help them learn appropriate "school" behaviors. Their early experiences may "not [have provided] . . . access to appropriate models, regular monitoring, regular academic and social success, and meaningful feedback . . . [their] early experiences are best characterized as infrequent, haphazard, and trial-and-error learning experiences" (Stormont, Lewis, Beckner, & Johnson, 2008, p. 2). Whether the poorly managed social experiences come from home life or early child care experiences will not matter to receiving teachers—we must meet the children where they are functioning and build upon their skills.

In this way, we stop the dreadful practice of exclusion of children on the basis of child behavior that often occurs due to absence of appropriate curricular structure. Failure to intervene in the early years leads to academic and social failure, and long-term mental health problems. Thus, it is critical that as teachers of young children we recognize symptoms and intervene for the healthy development of the children who present challenging behaviors, as well as for the life of their peers. As teachers, we expect to facilitate the development of people skills: i.e., the ability to get along with others, and the capacity to interact with peers and feel a part of the group. We provide scaffolding for children to successfully and appropriately manage emotions; model and develop cooperation skills and attitudes for successful working relationships with peers; reinforce each child's understanding of personal capacity to learn and to function in a group; and finally to show ways to adapt to new situations.

In high-quality schools, conscientious teachers pay attention to the development of the skills that all children need to be successful in school. Children need to learn how to tolerate frustration, share, play fair, and collaborate; they must be able to recognize times when they need to be quiet or can cheer loudly; they must be able to manage their anger, self-advocate, and adapt to personal space demands.

The most commonly used technique for managing challenging behavior requires skilled observation, data-based assessment, and carefully developed plans for individual children and their families. All teachers need to acquire the skills to use functional behavior assessment (FBA) as a technique to support the young children in their care. FBA is a procedure to identify the problem behavior and to implement ways to minimize and eliminate the challenging behavior (IRIS, 2016). This important tool—as well as a developmentally appropriate curriculum and classroom structure that supports an inclusive environment for all young children—assures that young children with challenging behaviors can learn to be successful young learners.

Prevention Works

One thing is clear: All teachers must be prepared for implementing special techniques as they are needed to support young children with challenging behaviors. To facilitate learning and promote social well-being, we must start early with our young charges. We must be prepared to persist over the long haul and to work collaboratively with families—supporting families with their priorities while mentoring the children for success in the life of school. Our best classrooms will feature caring communities and promote cooperation. In the primary years, we must also strive to support young learners with challenging behaviors in their strides toward the accomplishment of academic standards.

Conclusion

Child behaviors that teachers find exasperating, bothersome, aggravating, and grating disrupt learning for individual children as well as upset the instructional atmosphere for the group as a whole. Teachers must intervene when children present all variations of challenging behavior so that the classroom can be an effective community for learners and for teachers. Teachers are the leaders in the social world of school. They are responsible for mentoring young children in their classroom communities, where they will be required to acquire the skills, knowledge, and dispositions that will last them a lifetime. In the following chapters we will examine the structure of the classroom, the curriculum, the classroom management factors, and family collaboration and offer connections for setting the stage for lifelong learning for our youngest scholars. In addition, we will offer suggestions for the exceptions to the rule, i.e., the children whose behaviors stretch the usual and customary techniques, and who are at risk of academic failure.

Chapter 1 Activities

1. Picture yourself at the grocery store on a crowded weekend. You see lots of children. They are grabbing boxes, whining, running in the aisles, laughing, screaming, and bouncing in the grocery cart. Which of these behaviors annoy you? Which behaviors are challenging? Why do you think the children

are behaving in these ways? What are the caregivers doing to create or change the behaviors? Now, think of yourself at a park where children are playing on the slides and building in the sandbox. One group of children is chasing each other toward the sidewalk leading to a busy street, while another is calling each other names and beginning to push each other. Families are occasionally interacting with the children. Which of these behaviors annoy you? Which behaviors are challenging? Now think about the way the children will enter your classroom, based on these before-school experiences. How do your observations inform your thinking about the ways in which young children's behavior may "push your buttons"? What can you do proactively to maintain a calm demeanor as you help children develop self-control? What do you believe your role is in assisting with young children's behaviors beyond the classroom?

2. You value the idea of self-empowered learners at all ages. Andrea, a 7-year-old, comes to your class and for the first week seems prone to roaming the room and picking up notebooks and pencils from others' desks, all very silently. Initially, when Andrea says "sorry," the other children seem to take her behavior and apology in stride, but by week 4, they are becoming annoyed with Andrea and beginning to say, loudly, "that's mine," and "leave me alone." Which of Andrea's behaviors do you tackle first? How do you respond to the other children? Outline a way to uncover the meaning of her behavior. How will you coach Andrea? How might you use peer support?

3. Your best friend, Celine, is working at the Humpty Dumpty Child Care Center. She is finishing her degree in early childhood education while working there, so she works the early shift from 6:00 a.m. to 2:00 p.m. This means that she opens the center with the director, welcomes the children for breakfast, manages cleanup, and supervises the children's play. The center has 20 children by 7:00 a.m. Each morning the director goes into her office and begins paperwork. Charley, a 3-year-old, comes to the center every morning, half-asleep and crying. He wants to sit on Celine's lap. Celine loves the children and wants to reassure Charley, but she worries about

the other children who jump up and run to centers as soon as they gobble their breakfast. One day, Charlotte is enrolled in the center. She doesn't want breakfast, goes to the block corner, and starts throwing blocks against the wall. Celine tries to get the director's attention (who is now on the phone in her glass cubed-office), to no avail. Before Celine leaves for the day, she asks the director if Marigold can be asked to come in to help with the breakfast and play period. Even at 7:00 a.m. it would be helpful. The director says she can't afford to offer the hours to Marigold. After a week of this, Celine comes to you and says she is going to quit and go to work at a local department store, because she can't take it anymore. What advice do you give her? She is two semesters away from graduation.

2

Setting the Stage for Success

Kathleen M. Sheridan

This chapter looks at the classroom environment and the importance of deliberately setting up that environment for success. The discussion focuses on multiple aspects of the classroom environment, from the physical space to the social interactions, routines, and structures that are part of the overall environment. The chapter begins with a discussion about what is included in the classroom and how thoughtful planning for that environment can help teachers impact children in powerful ways. Included topics are the physical space, classroom materials and surfaces, personal interactions, conflict resolution, rules and rituals, developmentally appropriate guidance, PBIS, bullying, and successful teaching.

Classroom Environment

"Welcome to your new classroom!" One day, you will hear these words and you will be confronted with a multitude of decisions to make. For many of you, the decisions will need to be made quickly because many teachers are not hired or assigned their new classroom until just days before the start of the new school year. "Help!" is a common feeling when teachers are faced with this challenge. However, with some thought and planning ahead of time, you will have an arsenal of knowledge and tools to draw upon if this happens to you. The first place to start is with

FIGURE 2.1 Teacher greeting children for the beginning of the day.
Source: iStock

the bigger picture of the classroom setup, and that is the classroom environment. Your classroom environment has the potential to impact the children in your room in powerful ways. The classroom environment may temporarily overstimulate, bore, calm, or agitate those in it. Each of the children in your classroom comes with a unique personality, temperament, family culture, interests, likes, and dislikes. Some of your children will work better alone, some in groups. Some will be shy while others will be outgoing. Many will have had experiences that are different than the children around them. Creating a classroom environment that fits every child in your room should be your goal. This is not easy, but it is possible. This is critical because spending an extended period of one's life in an environment that works can help one to learn and thrive. However, spending an extended period of time that is unpleasant will eventually exact a toll (Curtis & Carter, 2015, p. 19). For example, if learners are easily distracted because the environment is too "busy" for them, they may trip over the legs of furniture or other children because they just don't "see" them. This is not only unsafe; it has the potential to create unnecessary conflict in the room. Likewise, if Adira has to sift through a large stack of mixed color construction paper to find the pink one, she may get frustrated and throw the whole stack on the floor, step on the unwanted pieces, and cry or scream in frustration. If Chun is allowed to take her book and read under a table with pillows and soft lighting, she may better comprehend what she is reading and have a deeper understanding of the material. If Sammy is allowed to work with Jacob on a project, he might learn more than he would on his own, and gain skills in collaboration and problem solving as well. As you can see, the environment or the "feeling" of the classroom matters!

The environment of the classroom also contributes to a child's understanding of "school" and anchors a young learner for success. If a child has built a personal schema of "school" as a place that is comfortable, welcoming, interesting, challenging, and caring, that child will be better situated to be ready to learn than the child whose schema of school is a place that is unsafe, threatening, uncomfortable, and boring. The environment is particularly important for young children who present with challenging behaviors. For these children, stability and assistance with navigating the social environment of the classroom might be essential for their success. For example, Darcy is a child who is rambunctious and often pushes or hits other children when excited, frustrated, or even just happy. Her pushing and hitting outbursts appear to happen the most when she is excited or when the classroom environment is chaotic, unpredictable, and unclear. Darcy's teacher has noticed that she is not chosen by the other children when playing and that when the other children make plans for after school play, Darcy is not invited to join them. The teacher and Darcy's parents have been working with her to identify and help her exhibit more socially acceptable behaviors when she is agitated or excited. These more acceptable behaviors are encouraged and reinforced throughout the school day and during trial play dates after school. The stability and consistency of the environment has been essential for Darcy to incorporate these new behaviors into her reactions, and she and the rest of the learning community will benefit from this.

So, how will you be able to assess whether your classroom environment is supportive for children? Use these four questions to self-assess whether your classroom environment will support children's behavior: 1) Is the environment predictable for children? 2) Do children know the behavioral expectations for the classroom? 3) Has appropriate classroom and playground behavior been acknowledged and reinforced, and has challenging behavior been acknowledged and mediated with helping children have access to the tools for exhibiting more socially acceptable behavior? and 4) Have you used data to make course corrections in your classroom environment? (Hancock & Carter, 2016, p. 67). This type of self-assessment is based on the Pyramid Model to building support for social-emotional learning in young children (Center on the Social and Emotional Foundations for Early Learning [CSEFEL], 2016). There are other instruments you can use to assess your classroom environment. Using one of the available instruments for self-assessment of the learning environment helps you be sure that you are making data-informed decisions about your environment and in the creation of action plans for improving your support of young learners.

In sum, the classroom environment sets the stage for learning. It can not only support the learning goals, but it can also assist in the facilitation of important social-emotional development. The environment of the classroom contributes to a child's understanding of "school" and sets the foundation for current and future success in the academic environment.

In the sections that follow I will discuss the importance of the physical structure of the classroom and the room arrangement. I will also discuss the classroom materials and how to organize them as well as the role that the classroom surfaces and displays play in creating an environment that will work for all of the children in your care. Finally, because the environment includes the ways that the people within the classroom interact and behave, I will focus on the social interactions, routines, and structures in the learning community that contribute to the overall classroom environment.

Classroom Space and Physical Environment

If you are like most new teachers, you will be excited when you receive your room assignment for the new school year. In fact, you probably already have a vision of what you want your new classroom to look like. However, that vision may be disrupted when you walk into your new room for the first time and realize that the layout of the room is not what you were planning on. Like most teachers, you do not have any influence on the architectural features of the space and they may not be to your liking. The walls, doors, and windows usually cannot be reconfigured. However, you can arrange the desks, tables, chairs, and learning centers to create a space that has a flow conducive to learning. Your classroom setup can have a major impact on your ability to manage the classroom and can help to create either a positive or negative classroom climate. Thus, you will want to spend some time developing a detailed plan for what you want your classroom arrangement to be and how that arrangement will help you achieve your teaching goals. As a start, take out some graph paper or sketch paper and experiment with different classroom arrangements. Settle on one that you believe works for you and your teaching style and educational philosophy. Then, continue reading and check to see if the arrangement you have sketched out addresses the concerns listed as important to consider. If not, redesign until you come up with a plan that is comprehensive and will meet your teaching goals. You may also wish to use an online tool that permits you to enter a sketch of your classroom such as Scholastic for Teachers.

An obvious first consideration for room arrangement is the traffic flow. The traffic pattern in your classroom is important for aesthetic reasons, but more importantly, it is important for safety and learning. For example, making sure that there is an open path to the doorway is essential for being sure that children can exit the room safely in an emergency. There should not be any area of the room that is arranged in such a manner that the children are not visible as you look around the room. All of the areas should be able to be reached without having to step over or disturb other children.

When thinking about how the children will move around from small group to large group and to lining up, think about the movement from the child's vantage point. Is it easy to move from place to place in the classroom? Does the organization and flow of the classroom traffic create a sense of belonging? Are the pathways wide enough so that children can move between centers alone and comfortably? If not, then LaTasha may brush into Juan as she passes from her seat at the math center to the story chair. This sets an opportunity for the two to engage in conflict.

Once you have figured out your traffic flow, you will want to consider what types of spaces to create in the classroom. Children should have spaces that allow for ample room to create, explore, move, play, listen, gather, and be quiet when necessary. There should be comfortable spaces where children can relax as well as more structured spaces where children perform specific tasks that need containment. This requires that your space and its arrangement are orderly and well thought out. A well designed and orderly room provides clues for children's behavior. For example, a large empty space with a tile floor will encourage children to run and move whereas a smaller contained space with a soft rug and books will encourage children to sit and lay to read or look at picture books. This supports children's sense of independence and self-reliance. It helps children make purposeful choices of materials and activities, and promotes task-centered focus that in turn fosters initiative in children and maximizes their potential learning.

It is also essential to plan how flexible you need your space to be. For example, will you need to reuse the central meeting space as a gross motor play area on a rainy day? If so, you will want to make sure that your furniture is portable and easy to move! The choices that you make about your classroom space will send a message to your students as well as to the parents and others who work in or visit the classroom. It will help communicate your teaching philosophy and values for your learning community. Make sure it is a good fit for your teaching style and that there is "some of you" in the design.

For example, many early childhood teachers incorporate some version of "learning centers" in their classroom design and setup. The research on knowledge acquisition and learning in the early childhood classroom supports the concept of learning centers but there is a wide variability in how a learning center can be designed. In the next section are some ideas and information to help you make a decision about what type of learning center design you will want to incorporate.

Setting Up Learning Centers

One way to be sure to support children in their work at learning centers is to be sure that they are set up to support social interaction. For example, if the center is designed for four children, the chairs should be arranged around a table, rather than in a line against the wall so children can talk about their work and support each other in completing suggested tasks. Be sure that the materials at the center are open-ended, so that the use of them promotes conversation. When children are working in centers, be sure that they know you are watching them and can be called upon to help mediate, if necessary. You and the children can put up signs that indicate how many children can be in each of the centers or you can use sign-ups as a reservation system for participation. If the goal is that every child visits a center, you will need check sheets for completion of tasks as a record of visits by each child to each center. With younger children, you may just want to keep track of where the children go so that you can see their interests. Commonly, centers are organized by subject and activity. For example, in kindergarten, a block center, art center, writing center, and a math and science center are the usual staples. In all classrooms, the centers need to reflect the curriculum and vary throughout the year. Shown in Figure 2.2 is an example of a classroom with centers lining the walls.

FIGURE 2.2 Early childhood classroom with centers.

Classroom Materials

You will also need to consider what learning materials and technology you will have available in the classroom and how you will make them accessible to the children in your room. For example, will there be laptops, iPads, mp3 players, or SMART boards for the children to utilize during work time? If so, are they portable and available for the whole class or will children need to take turns using them? What other types of learning materials will you choose to have available in the classroom? Will they be stored so that they are visible and accessible to all children? In making classroom materials visible and accessible you will foster independence in children and will also encourage children to make purposeful choices.

When you purposefully choose and organize exciting and appropriate materials, you promote interest, curiosity, and intellectual challenge. Organization promotes order and ownership of the shared space, materials, and work areas. If children are interested and challenged, if they feel ownership, your teaching goals and the learning that goes on in the classroom will be enhanced. Additionally, the materials you choose as well as their accessibility will also impact your lesson planning, so it is essential to make a plan for the access to and use of materials.

You also want to make sure that any materials that you do have available are in good working order. All of the materials should be properly functioning and cared for. This shows that you respect the children in your classroom and that you also respect the learning environment and the materials themselves. You might consider allowing the children to be involved in their upkeep because involving children in the care of materials promotes citizenship and independence and helps to create a classroom community.

Your materials should also be chosen carefully so that they reflect the children's gender, religious, racial, and ethnic backgrounds. Make sure to ask yourself if the material is thoughtfully representative of the cultural traditions, community history, music, art, language, and literature of all of the children in your classroom. It is important to consider whether the materials you have available for the children represent authentic perspectives on race, family structures, gender, religion, and socioeconomic background rather than stereotypical or historically inaccurate presentations of diversity (Saifer, Edwards, Ellis, Ko, & Stuczynski, 2011). For example, in a classroom visit I completed a couple of weeks ago, I saw a learning center in a second grade classroom that had materials that were meant to be representative of children in Japan. When I went over to the center, I was surprised to see wooden shoes and kimonos as well as Chinese paper and calligraphy pens. Little in this group of materials was reflective of Japanese school children today—and Chinese and Japanese cultures were lumped together as one group! This type of thoughtless and inappropriate choice of learning materials is unfortunate and does not represent the learning and knowledge of curriculum, culture, and diversity that teachers must have.

Finally, to prevent the spread of germs and save you and the children in your classroom from frequent illnesses and sick days, the materials should be regularly sanitized and cleaned. I cannot stress this enough, **clean and sanitize** the materials that will be shared among the children in your classroom. Germs can live on surfaces and children carry around a lot of germs on their hands. You will save yourself (and the children in your room) many sick days and colds by engaging in a weekly sanitizing routine of shared materials and table and desk tops.

Take a look at the lists of common materials for the early childhood classroom in the chart in Table 2.1 and create a list for your own classroom:

TABLE 2.1 List of common materials

Art	Music	Literacy	Math	Science	Dramatic Play	Blocks and Accessories	Technology
Crayons, pencils, and markers	Musical instruments	Letter puzzles, word cards with and without pictures, letter cubes, and word games	Unifix cubes, 10 frames, rods, and other cubes	Sensory table materials such as water, sand, dirt, beans and other materials suitable for scooping and pouring	Quality dress-up clothes	Wooden unit blocks of various shapes	Digital cameras
Scissors	CD players and CDs or streaming music for listening and playing out loud	Books, posters, and magazines	Counters of various types and dice	Scoops, strainers, sifters, measuring cups, and other materials for digging, pouring and scooping	Dolls (make sure dolls are both male and female and are of multiple types of race and ethnic makeups)	Block accessories such as vehicles, farm, zoo, ocean, and other animals, pretend insects, traffic signs and pretend people	Computers
Papers of different types and sizes	Props for movement such as scarves and ribbons	Puppets and pretend telephones	Sorting materials	Magnets, magnifying glasses, prisms, and binoculars	Housekeeping furniture such as a toy sink, stove, oven, bed or cradle, high chair, and refrigerator	Keys, maps, cardboard tubes, and other found materials	Tablets such as iPads and Kindles
Collage materials (sequins, yarn, buttons, cotton balls, etc.)	Noise makers	Flannel and magnetic boards with letters and flannel story pieces	Pattern blocks, attribute blocks, and pattern boards	Science games such as animal bingo, matching sounds, feely bags, and gears	Eating utensils, dishes, pots and pans, and pretend food	Foam, plastic, and other types of blocks	Printers

Play dough, clay, and tools such as rolling pins, wooden hammers, etc.	Pencils and other writing implements	Shape puzzles	Objects found in nature such as shells, rocks, leafs, minerals, feathers, pinecones, and seeds	Child-size props for cleaning such as mops, brooms, dustpans, a vacuum, sponges, dishcloths, and dusters	iPods and docking stations
Glue bottles and glue sticks	Papers of various types including lined and unlined and graph paper	Magna tiles		Props such as a cash register, telephone, clocks and timers, etc.	Bluetooth speakers
Paint, easel, and brushes	Envelopes	Pegs and peg boards		Prop boxes for various themed play	Keyboards, and other types of accessories
Materials to make multi-dimensional projects such as empty boxes, coffee filters, cardboard tubes, straws, etc.	Name cards of the children in the classroom community	Lacing cards and patterns			
		Math games			

Classroom Surfaces and Displays

Once the "box"—that is, the classroom space—is organized, you will want to think about using the walls, cabinet tops, and other surfaces for displays. Ask yourself if there are certain items that will be consistently displayed and updated. For example, is there a space for families to check to see important notes? Can the children see the daily schedule and know where to look for it? Is the schedule graphic regularly updated, showing specials that occur, as well as the ways the class has differing demands throughout the year? For all displays, consider the purpose: Why have you placed that poster, drawing, or collection of artifacts there?

There are many reasons for displaying items in your classroom. Some possibilities include encouraging curiosity, celebrating the contribution of the children in your classroom, documenting class or individual student learning and progress, and celebrating family collaboration with the class and building community. You will want to make sure that the display items correlate and change with the curriculum. You might want to let the children help to choose or create certain displays in the room and you will want to be sure to keep your displays fresh. A display or sign that is always there and not updated will be one that becomes "part of the wallpaper" and eventually will not be noticed or seen by the children or by you!

While the environment starts with the physical structure of the room and includes the organization of materials and the overall atmosphere of the classroom, it also includes the ways the people within the classroom community will interact and behave. The interpersonal interactions that occur in the class can support child development and add to a child's sense of security and feelings of safety or they can create barriers and inhibitors for child progress. Therefore, there are baseline expectations for structuring the personal interactions of the class community as well as important ways to individualize and to support and teach new skills for young children with challenging behavior.

Personal Interactions

A foundational underpinning of teacher-child interactions is your knowledge of the children whom you are teaching. In particular, you will want to know about the cultural and social traditions and experiences of the individuals in your classroom community. To see and

FIGURE 2.3 Children working together.
Source: iStock

understand young children, whether in play or academic settings, observation of their behavior is a key tool. In their work products and their conversations with peers you may see how they represent their knowledge, their self, their family, and their thoughts about their social world. Their perceptions and understandings of race, ethnicity, and social class can be observed when looking at the peers whom they choose to socialize with, as well as their direct comments and the responses you see when presenting photos and discussing history, children's literature, and current events. This observational data will assist you in determining your classroom climate for inclusion as well as respect for each individual within the class community (Derman-Sparks, Ramsey, & Edwards, 2011). Besides the consideration of social class, race, and ethnicity, gender is an important variable with underlying perceptions and beliefs based on a young child's experiences in family and community situations.

You have the chance to promote positive interactions across genders by helping young children communicate, play cooperatively, and to learn about each other. This positive interaction can occur as you plan small group activities and permit boys and girls to engage together in non–gender typical activities, such as boys caring for the babies or playing with dolls in the house or dramatic play center, and girls building skyscrapers and tunnels in the block center. In fact, try not to use the gendered terms "girl" and "boy" when referring to children and instead use gender-neutral terms such as "children" and "friends." Through this thoughtful way of addressing and communicating with children, you are communicating that boys and girls can be friends and are refusing to accept gender-specific comments such as girls can't be super-heroes or boys cannot care for babies. By encouraging children to interact with each other on attributes other than gender, you foster cross-gender interaction habits for young children. To develop consideration for gender neutral interaction, use curriculum materials in nonstereotypical ways. For example, encourage boys to be involved in cooking and girls to use trucks and cars. In addition, group children with both genders in science tasks and reading activities. These practices help young children develop respect for each other and learn about each other to form positive attitudes across gender lines (Manaster & Jobe, 2012).

At the beginning of the year, or when new children are added to your class, you will want to know children's personal interests and passions in addition to the basic demographic and academic data that you will have available. Establishing a personal relationship with each child requires conversation, careful observation, and collaboration with each child's family. One critical step in establishing relations with individuals is to be fully present when listening to a child speaking to you. Are you at Sydnie's eye level? Can Sky see that you are paying attention to his story or request? Your behavior models the act of listening and attending to children, which is an important skill that they can use with you and with their peers.

Personal relationships comprise the bedrock of promoting child behaviors. Through your actions as a teacher and learning community member, you promote and enhance six life skills that all children need: attachment, belonging, self-regulation, collaboration, contribution, and adaptability (Bilmes, 2012).

Your relationship with individual children sets the tone and is a model for children to follow. These skills are developed through the personal interactions that you have one-on-one with each child and as you set up your community for child-to-child interactions. When the children in the classroom hear you encourage participation of all learners and see you accept a child's errors with acceptance, kindness, and humor, and as an important part of the learning process, they will begin to model these behaviors with each other.

At the beginning of the year, or when new children join the classroom community, it is important to help children learn about each other. This can be accomplished through teacher-and-child conversation that focuses on favorite colors, favorite TV programs, favorite books, sports played, musical instruments played, and so on. These getting-acquainted activities should be based on the children's developmental level, with questions for younger children developed in casual conversation around small group activities.

In child care settings and schools, young children should have many opportunities to form friendships. At the very least, however, they must learn to interact in the social atmosphere of the classroom. The classroom is where they will spend many hours throughout the rest of their lives. If they are unsuccessful with social relationships in the early years, they may be perceived by classmates as "bad" or "not friends." Then, this may result in Yasmine, Richard, or Eli having to fight their tendency to reject children and to demonstrate a stereotypical response toward the "bad" or "not friends" children for the rest of their elementary years. Richard, Yasmine, and Eli know that they should include all of their peers in activities and treat them in a friendly manner; however, if Harold is perceived as mean due to his poorly developed social skills, they may indeed be frustrated and reluctant to include Harold or Evan or Martha. For example, "I don't want to sit next to Evan; he is not my friend" or "You took my toy, so you are not invited to my birthday party." These stereotypical responses can hinder positive social interactions at all ages of a child's educational path and have long-term negative impacts on feelings of belonging and on actual learning.

For children presenting challenging behavior in early childhood settings, the stakes are particularly high, since your response as a teacher may have life-altering effects on the child. Teachers who problem-solve and figure out ways to intervene and support children will contribute to their development as successful scholars. Additionally, young children often come to child care and school with limited large-group experience, so it is here that the challenging behavior's effect may be more readily noticed and problematic. The research that supports early identification, socialization, and inclusion in the early years as important for all children indicates that the use of inclusion principles to guide teachers' work is particularly important with children.

The *DEC Recommended Practices for Enhancing Services for Young Children with Disabilities and Their Families* (2015) summarizes and explains current research to guide best practices for young children with disabilities. Best practice suggests that including young children with disabilities in the mainstream classroom is a powerful way for children to learn acceptance of others. When teachers are successful in implementing personal interactions to support inclusive attitudes among children, all the children will feel a sense of belonging and membership; practice positive social relationships and develop friendships; and grow to reach their full potential (Favazza, Ostrosky, & Mouzourou, 2016, p. 5). In addition to teacher work to support young children with disabilities, all children benefit from teachers who practice a culturally responsive approach. Therefore, extending these practices to all children and applying the principles to your classroom will assure optimum development for all of the young children and families that you serve. Research informs us that

> Learning styles, like the language we speak and the skin we wear, are not separate entities to be "fixed" but part of the essential nature of any human being. If we can see all of the children we teach—skin color, culture, learning styles, income level notwithstanding—as complete, deserving, brilliant human beings, then perhaps we will manage to create the educational system we need. Education for all children should be "special"—that is, specially designed to discover the strengths and accommodate the needs of each child.
>
> (Delpit, 2013, p. 103)

Responsive adult-child interactions are important in particular, especially those that show sensitivity, responsiveness, and contingency. That is, your interactions should be authentic and personalized for each child, and on target for that child's perceptions of needed support. You will want to be on the lookout to ensure that your interactions are reciprocal and that you follow the child's lead. Your response should make sense to the child. If you are unsure whether the child understands, try to put yourself in the child's shoes. How would you feel if your teacher responded to you in that same manner? If your answer is "sad," "powerless," "confused" or any other negative response, change your interaction. Try asking open-ended questions or using open-ended responses to get a clearer understanding of the child's reasoning. For example, when you see Jerome going over to the display wall and ripping down the drawing he created, instead of yelling for him to "stop" and chastising him, you might instead quietly go over to him, move down to his eye level, and say "Louis, your drawing made me so happy when I looked at it hanging on the wall. The colors made me want to dance. Why did you rip it down?" Louis might explain that his friend was making fun of him for it, or that his sister Aidenn had drawings on the refrigerator at home and he wanted to bring it home to have one of his up as well. No matter his reasoning, even if he responds by stating "I don't know," a thoughtful and caring interaction with you will help you to understand Louis better and perhaps help him to think of a more appropriate behavior in the future. Each interaction you have with a child can be profoundly important to that child and to your learning community. Careful reflection on situations that puzzle you or seem off will help you be more responsive. Personal interactions are critically important to all young children for later developmental progress (McCollum, 2015, pp. 87–97).

The social construction of the classroom is critical since our society is increasingly diverse and young children will have frequent contact with others whose families have various constellations of adults as primary caregivers; the divorce rate is high and social-class variation can be extreme in some situations. These diversities are represented in racial, language, ethnic, and religious differences within classrooms. Delpit (2013) says to teachers:

> Your work does matter more than you can imagine. Your students, particularly if they are low-income children of color, cannot succeed without you. You are their lifeline to a better future. If you put energy and expertise into your teaching, learn from those who know your students best, make strong demands, express care and concern, engage your students, and constantly ensure that your charges are capable of achieving (this describes a "warm demander" teacher), then you are creating for your students as Professor Bill Trent once said about his own warm demander teachers, "a future we could not even imagine for ourselves."
>
> (p. 88)

The quality of your personal interactions with young children can be observed with the *Classroom assessment scoring system* (CLASS) (Pianta,

La Paro, & Hamre, 2008). CLASS is based on developmental theory and research that was developed with the foundational assumption that the interactions between children and adults are the primary mechanisms for student development and learning (Pianta et al., 2008, p. 1). The scoring system includes three domains for indicating quality of early childhood programs: emotional support, classroom organization, and instructional support. Thus, as you think about setting up your classroom for children's success through your personal interactions, the dimension of emotional support is also critical. Important elements of support for motivating young children, and promoting emotional and social support, include the demonstration of a classroom positive climate, sensitivity to each child's emotional and academic concerns, and consideration for the child's interests, motivations, and points of view (p. 3). The classroom organization variables include the ways in which you as a teacher manage behavior, assure productivity in learning, provide interesting activities, and promote engaged learning. Instructional support includes your careful crafting of discussions, appropriate and timely feedback, and the effective way that you model and support language development (Pianta et al., 2008). If a CLASS observer is in your classroom to assess the learning environment, they will score each of these dimensions on a rating scale and determine your progress in each area. Pay attention to the kinds of questions and conversations you have with children. Scaffold their learning and bring real-life examples and conversations into your interactions. Make sure that there are opportunities for children to learn, and be flexible enough to allow children to have a voice in what and how the learning progresses in the classroom. Be genuine and warm when welcoming the children in your classroom. Acknowledge them and create opportunities for using new language as well as demonstrating language for them. In other words, be a teacher!

An important element for promoting self-reliance in children is the teaching of social skills and ways to approach problem solving in social issues. "Problem solving allows children to stay calm during difficult situations, repair social relations quickly, and get their needs met in ways that are safe and fair" (Joseph & Strain, 2010, p. 39). You must help children identify social problems as they arise and pose some solutions for resolution. Help them to analyze what should happen next if a particular solution is implemented. Encourage them to try the solution and then reflect upon its effectiveness. If the solution did not work, assist them in refining or retrying a new solution. This technique should be taught, integrated in the curriculum, and used to solve common classroom issues between peers and for the group. For example, Jasmine noticed that you had only one new iPad for a lesson that you were implementing and that there were four children who need to use it for their work. When she tells you about the dilemma ask her to help you solve it. Say, "what should we do? How can we resolve this situation?" Or, if Ollie tells you that he forgot his pink marker and tried to borrow Charlie's he may say Charlie said "No" when asked what happened. Help him to figure out what other solutions there might be in addition to borrowing Charlie's marker. Scaffold his thinking to come to a successful solution. It is through problem solving among and between peers and in other classroom peer interactions that children acquire social skills and develop a sense of self-efficacy.

> In developing friendships, children learn important cognitive skills, such as perspective taking, problem solving, and pattern recognition (such as in turn taking). By practicing conflict and negotiation in safe relationships, children learn to feel sympathy for and empathy with others and build their friendship skills. When children learn about emotions and practice identifying and using them, they learn to focus and redirect negative emotions.
>
> (Gallagher, 2013, p. 32)

When interacting with children, teachers often assume that praise is an important tool. Guidelines for effective praise suggest that the praise contain specific information about what was done well. Praise should not compare children and should be used to recognize partial steps or compliance with the goal for the behavioral expectation. When Misia comes up to you and shows you her new creation, responding by comparing it to Yoram's creation is not only inappropriate, but it can also have a negative impact on both Yoram and Misia. If children are also provided with a self-reflection guide, the praise can help them see where they are meeting social expectations and where they need to go next. This is one of the tools that can be helpful for children who present challenging behavior.

For young children who present challenging behavior, peer modeling may be an effective tool. Pairing Theo with Judah to complete a project might help Judah to learn ways to respond in a quicker and more efficient manner to a math problem. Theo can be asked to reflect on the way the two of them accomplished the math problem together. Buddy play is another version of this approach to teach children appropriate social behavior. It is a

> three-step process: stay, play and talk. Children are assigned as buddies, [and asked to] go to the center where your buddy wants to play. [The children are encouraged to] share, take turns and ask their buddy to play. . . . [They are also encouraged to] converse with your buddy about the play or about the buddy.
> (Gallagher, 2013, p. 31)

Besides a focus on verbal interactions, you should be aware of the non-verbal perspectives that exist. Cultural backgrounds play a role in determining appropriate personal space, eye contact, and silence, as well as whether smiling can be trusted and whether adults should physically guide a child's hands. Watching facial expressions, and recognizing the body language of engagement, distress, and boredom, are helpful for understanding the interpersonal interactions between children as well as with the teacher. These non-verbal interactions are particularly important when young children have limited language, either because they are learning English, or have difficulty in thinking linguistically or saying what they want or need. When children cannot communicate, they become frustrated and resort to either giving up—that is, not participating at all—or by screaming, tearing up materials, etc. Think about how you would feel in a group of peers if you were the only one who could not communicate through language. I recently had the experience of traveling to France. I do **not** speak any French and can understand very little of it. I felt totally isolated at times, and I found myself being very quiet and not even trying to communicate. I would drift off into my own world of thought because I was separated from the others through language. However, when a French acquaintance tried to include me, using gestures, broken English, and body language, I reengaged and tried hard to communicate and understand. This happens with the children in your classroom, too. The use of formal or informal sign language or electronic language boards may support social interaction among peers, as well as between child and teacher.

Inevitably in social situations in the classroom, whether sharing space and materials or working together on a project, conflict may occur: Therefore, the personal interactions of the class community must include ways to resolve conflict.

Conflict Resolution

Since children will have conflicts in the classroom—over sharing materials, use of space, need for privacy, and so on—you will need to include problem-solving strategies to help them solve the problem. If the problem is serious or if the children are still learning how to solve personal issues, these six steps can be helpful: 1) showing a calm demeanor, stop any hurtful actions, such as hitting or name calling; 2) label and recognize the individual children's feelings; 3) find out what happened to set off the conflict; 4) identify the problem to be solved; 5) ask the children to figure out next actions toward a solution and have all involved agree on one; 6) watch the resolution being carried out and scaffold for success, as needed (Evans, 2002). In all cases, as the teacher, you must assure the safety of the children and intervene when a child is unable to stop a dangerous behavior.

FIGURE 2.4 Child pouting because his friends wouldn't share . . . a conflict to solve.
Source: iStock

One practical strategy used by a kindergarten teacher is "talking chairs." At the beginning of the school year, Mr. Neimark (2015) sets up two chairs in the middle of the room with stuffed animals seated upon them. He tells the children these chairs can be used to discuss disagreements and provides "talking pieces" (such as a ball, animal, or block) that the children can use to designate whose turn it is to talk. To use the chairs, the children must follow three rules: 1) take turns, only one person can talk at a time—the person with the talking piece; 2) each tells what they think is the problem and describes their feelings about the problem; 3) they agree on a decision and record agreement on a kindness chart (p. 110). For example, Niv and Jamari were in conflict because Jamari kept running into Niv's play space in the dramatic play area. Niv was yelling at Jamari, "Stay away from where I am playing." Jamari kept laughing and teasing Niv by continuing to disrupt her play. The teacher encouraged the children to go to the talking chairs to try to resolve their conflict. Niv and Jamari went to the chairs. Niv talked first while Jamari listened to her tell him that his interruptions and intrusions bothered her. Then, Jamari took the "talking piece" (a stuffed animal) and told Niv that he really wanted to play with her, but because she would not let him, he was feeling sad and bothering her. He asked Niv if he could play with her. Niv agreed that he could join her if he wanted to play what she was playing, and if he would be a good listener and not try to ruin what she was doing. Jamari enthusiastically agreed and they went back to the dramatic play area to continue their play.

Another approach for conflict resolution is the creation of a "peace place." A "peace place" is a quiet, out-of-the-way spot where children can choose to work out their problems. Some possible materials to include in your "peace place" include an unbreakable mirror to see what facial expressions are like; puppets; play dough or other sensory materials to express emotions; a rain stick to be used as a talking stick so that the children can take turns talking to one another without interruption; soothing music; feelings posters; and soft chairs (Lamm, Grouix, Hansen, Patton, & Slaton, 2006, pp. 22–28). Children can elect to go to this space to solve problems between themselves. It is a space where the children choose to go after they have learned about its purpose and you have demonstrated how to use it. Some effective demonstration strategies include role playing with small groups about how the space can be used and puppet shows enacting the use of the space. Readings from children's books can also be used to illustrate the kinds of problems to be solved. The readings are often a supplement to the ideas that children suggest when the modeling of the peace place is developed.

The Social Emotional and Cognitive Understanding and Regulation in education (SECURe) program (Bailey, Jones, Jacob, Madden, & Phillips, 2012) uses a "taking turns bag" to assist in resolving conflicts over the use of a toy or equipment. The bag contains a coin and a timer; the children flip the coin to determine who goes first. They then agree on a time limit and set the timer for the sharing. This technique is child-driven, but first modeled and demonstrated by the teacher. Using these conflict resolution approaches with concrete objects and steps helps children learn to manage conflict not only in the classroom, but also in community and home situations. Besides conflict between two children, there are situations where conflict may occur within groups of children.

If many children are having problems with conflict about an issue or on a particular day, a group discussion can elicit solutions by the children. For example, Ms. Donohue sits in a circle to discuss the second-grade girls' perception that the boys always claim the football at recess. She asks the children for potential solutions. The class agrees on a protocol for solving the issue. They decide that the girls can choose the football first one day and the boys first on another. The children agree that this is a fair practice. The conflict with associated hurt feelings is solved by the children, which empowers them to think that they can solve social issues among themselves.

You might also read a story about other children who are having a class problem, if the issue is a particularly sensitive one. This approach may work well when a group of children are picking on a particular child or children. Table 2.2 lists some popular children's books to consider using with the children in your classroom.

TABLE 2.2 Popular children's books

Title	Author
No, it's mine	Shimrit Nothman and Bushra Owais (Illustrator)
It's mine!	Leo Lionni
The Butter Battle book	Dr. Seuss
Words are not for hurting	Elizabeth Verdick

Children's literature can often assist in resolving conflict. The story or real situation written down and told in story form can remove the conflict from the "right now" to the position of the conflict happening elsewhere with other children and show how others solved the problem.

Besides the specific techniques, it is helpful to remember three principles for helping children resolve conflicts: 1) Appear calm in conflict situations as you show through your language, body language, tone of voice, and facial expression; this approach assures children that they are safe in a contested situation; 2) assure the children that they can solve the conflict—the problem is theirs to own and solve; provide safety support, as necessary, removing a hitting child, if the child cannot stop the behavior; 3) believe in the competence of the children to solve the problems, providing reminder scaffolding as necessary (DeVries & Zan, 2012, pp. 85–86). Take a look at the following (adapted from DeVries & Zan, 2012, p. 86) list of specific suggestions for using these principles.

- Helping children develop the language for expressing their feelings and attitudes.
- Helping children get to the meat of an issue by restating the problem in terms they can understand.
- Allowing children to reject proposed solutions so that the conflict is resolved mutually.
- Proposing solutions for the conflict when the children seem unable to do so.

For older children, you can scaffold the vocabulary and their understanding of "conflict" by using their words and putting them on a graphic organizer chart. You can ask questions such as, what is a conflict? What kinds have conflict have you experienced? What does "conflict" mean to you? (Kriedler, 1994). Then, to move the discussion to situations that are not personal, you can read children's literature and listen for appropriate solutions modeled in the story. Some questions to consider are: "Who was involved? What was the conflict about? When did it happen? Where did it happen? Why was there a conflict? How did the conflict turn out? How might the conflict have been prevented?" (Kriedler, 1994, p. 16). Through this process you can provide the opportunity to help children identify ways to recognize situations that may create conflict and to solve the situations. Table 2.3 lists some examples of popular children's books that might be used for this story session.

TABLE 2.3 Popular children's books

Book Title	Author
Let's be enemies	Janice May Udry
The quarreling book	Charlotte Zolotow
Matthew and Tilly	Rebecca C. Jones
Alexander and the terrible, no good, very bad day	Judith Viorst

Besides using literature to promote the development of social skills, there is a specialized technique developed by Gray (1996) to assist young children with autism in learning to function in social situations. The technique is called *social stories,* and when boiled down to its essential elements, forms a social script for a particular situation. In addition, the script is often illustrated with pictures. For example, a social story may be built around, "What do I do when I want to join a group working on a science project?" Each step should be articulated and outlined for the child, and will need to match the child's specific needs. That is, it will be necessary to consider some of the complexities from the specific child's perspective. For instance, does the child have a history of being disruptive and thus feared by peers? Does she speak? Does he love science? Is there a peer that can help the child enter their group? The answers to these and other questions will shape the steps for developing the story, i.e., the steps that the child must follow to enter the group. Thus, while it sounds as if the technique might be simple to implement, it is in fact complex since the story must meet the child's goal, be understandable by the child, and contain the appropriate cues to match the task.

Each of the specialized techniques to support children presenting challenging behavior are elaborations of ways early childhood teachers powerfully affect the lives of individual children. These are the personal interactions that "intentionally connect with the child while at the same time saying or doing something to guide the child's learning a small step forward" (Dombro, Jablon, & Stetson, 2011, p. 13). Through these personalized interactions, teachers use the learning opportunities that are available in the classroom, facilitate the development of child friendships and adjustment to the social world of the school, and promote enjoyment of school. In these ways, teachers model and facilitate a holistic approach to learning that encourages problem solving, curiosity, and reflection, as well as facilitating the development of the necessary social skills to navigate the world of school. In addition to the one-on-one small group focus on the development and elaboration of personal interactions and social competence, teachers must also plan social structures for the whole class that ensures the development of community. One such technique is the morning meeting.

Morning Meetings

Kriete and Davis (2014) describe an approach to class meetings with the intention of anchoring the community relationships of students. They describe the morning meeting as the central all-class meeting to beginning each school day. The morning meeting is used to foster class communication and collaboration as well as social-emotional learning through the regular practice of social skills as well as linguistic development and critical thinking skills.

The morning meeting approach has four segments. Morning meetings start with a welcome where children greet each other by name and may include singing, clapping, handshaking, or other salutations. Next there is a sharing time where children share and discuss news, thoughts, feelings, and ideas to set a positive climate for the day. Third there is some type of group activity where children interact with each other to build collaboration, and finally, the morning meeting usually concludes with news and announcements where children read, write, recite, and discuss the daily message, as well as learn about the events for the day (p. 3). For the youngest children, the morning meeting should be short and match the development of the children in the room. For slightly older children, the meeting can last as long as 30 minutes if the children are developmentally ready for longer periods of whole group engagement. Morning meetings build community through fostering skills for listening, attention, cooperative interaction, and expression. This practice represents an investment in the development of peer and teacher relationships. These meetings require careful and thoughtful planning and development while paying close attention to the children, routines, and rules for collaboration in the classroom.

Class Meetings

A class meeting is different from a morning meeting because the class meeting is usually more focused on solving problems or issues within the class. Class meetings offer an opportunity for talking through

FIGURE 2.5 Class meeting.
Source: iStock

classroom issues and individual feelings in a safe environment. As the teacher, you will want to structure the class meeting so that feelings and thoughts are shared without judgment about the content of the information shared or the children who share it. Through these experiences children learn respect and care for each other. Respect can be built through turn-taking and you can help children to see not only their own point of view, but also those of other children. For example, some common problems to be solved with a class meeting include issues such as name-calling, arguments, taking toys/equipment from others without permission, excluding others from play, not taking turns, and not sharing. When you are planning a class meeting, remember that ground rules are important. You may want to establish expectations for successful interactions in the group meeting. Appropriate expectations can be developed by the children with your assistance and might include rules such as: Each child must sit and listen while another child is talking, or everyone who wants to should have a chance to share. You will also need to decide what happens when the rules are not followed. For example, you might decide that any child who is not following the rules will be required to move away from the meeting until they are ready to engage in the meeting in a manner that is conducive to the group expectations and success (Vance & Weaver, 2002, p. 31). These are ground rules that children can easily grasp and should be worded in a positive and constructive manner.

In addition to classrooms and classroom meetings, all other group situations need rules so that there are clear expectations set for all participants. In addition, rules promote a sense of security for the children and help to create a structure for the class so that the classroom is perceived as a safe environment.

Rules and Rituals in School

When children enter child care centers and school situations, they encounter rules for behaving in the class and school community. The rules in school are designed to preserve order and promote safety for the group and the individuals. Good and Good (2008) identified four general management principles that apply to the development of rules: 1) children will follow rules they understand and respect; 2) meaningful curricular activities engage children and minimize rule infractions; 3) the rules should create a space for learning rather than focus on misbehavior; and 4) the goal for class rules is to help children learn self-control rather than rely on teacher control over them (p. 77). These rules are usually more formal than those in families and often have less flexibility for negotiated observance. For example, walking on the right side of the hallway in a school building is a customary rule. But, what if you have a child who does not yet know right from left? How will you help this child to follow the rule? Another common rule is that there is no running in hallways, even if you are excited to be at school for the day. How will you help children to regulate their behavior so that they can comply with the rules? In addition, lines are a ubiquitous feature of schools—lining up to enter the building, lining up to go to lunch, lining up to go to recess. How will you help the children to form a line and stay in line without bumping into one another, pushing one another, and "budging in line"? Each of these required behaviors represent developmental challenges for all young children and especially for those who may have challenges with impulse control.

Let's examine how you might help young children with walking on the right side of the hall. To structure this activity for success, you may wish to remind the children that the class banner (or some other visible symbol) is on the right side, as they leave the room, so they will walk down the hall with the banner waving good-bye to them. Upon their return, the banner will be waving hello on the left side of the hall. No running in the halls can be especially challenging for children who are excited to get to their intended location or are invigorated by a long hallway that looks perfect for running. You might create the simple rule that "inside we walk everywhere." This rule is much easier for children to remember than trying to remember that they do not run in the hallway and the classroom and the music room and the computer lab. In the case of lining up, the variable to prepare for is that of spatial understanding: How close should I be to my friend in line? Arm's distance? Elbow's distance? Setting up expectations, and practicing for success, reduces potential for conflict.

Once inside the classroom, the community will need rules to govern the social life of the classroom. In keeping with developmentally appropriate practice, the rules should be designed to support children's learning of self-control. In addition, the children should be involved in setting up the rules and any infractions should have known logical consequences. As described by Brady, Forton, Porter, and Wood (2003) the process of establishing rules with children accomplishes several goals: It promotes investment in the rules for the community, gives signposts for appropriate social behavior, establishes boundaries for safety, and promotes understanding of citizenship responsibilities (p. 22). The process for rule setting with this philosophy for school-age children begins with a facilitated discussion of child and family goals for the year. Then the development of rules begins, with an emphasis on the positive, and finally narrows down to just a few rules (p. 22). Once the classroom rules are set, it is a good idea to share them with families. In this way, school and family collaboration is facilitated.

In thinking about rules, fewer is better—three to five—with a focus on what is needed for preserving order. Figure 2.6 shows an example of common rules that are posted in classrooms for the children to see.

I listen while others are talking.
I take turns.
I keep my hands and feet and objects to myself.
I work hard.
I respect myself and others.

Figure 2.6 Classroom Rules.

Note that these rules are framed in the first person, which shows children that each of them can be responsible for their own personal behavior. Also, note that there are only five rules, making it possible to call children's attention to the shared responsibility for the climate and order in the class, as well as promoting easy observance and potential for conformance to the harmony of the community.

In establishing rules, best practice suggests that you enlist the children's help in creating the rules. Use positive statements about what the children will do rather than negative statements about what is forbidden. "No talking" sets a different tone than "I listen while others are talking." Make sure that you explain each of the rules and rehearse compliance with them. Then, you will need to reinforce observance of the rules. As the days go by, if the rules are to work, you will want to practice them with the children. What does it mean to respect, take turns, and listen? Practicing can involve you modeling the rules, using scenarios for discussion, and discussing the rules at meeting times. When scenarios are used, include feelings. For example, you can ask, "What did it feel like when Zoe pulled your paper out of your hand?" or "How did you feel when you realized that you interrupted Kendra?"

In addition to setting up the rules and practicing them, the children will need to know what happens if a rule is broken. You can explain the way that rule infractions will result in logical and natural consequences and help children to come up with appropriate consequences. Often times, young children come up with punitive and inappropriate consequences for rule infractions, so gentle guidance on your part will most likely be necessary. For example, young children may decide that the consequence for running in the hallway is no recess for a whole week. Since this consequence is neither natural or logical, you will have to guide children to a more logical consequence.

In conjunction with basic rules that develop community and smooth social function, rituals can promote group cohesion and affinity. The intentional use of traditions—such as welcoming new classmates, celebratory family dinners, and ceremonies commemorating milestones—can foster belonging, connection, and shared values for the class community (Howell & Reinhard, 2015). In addition to rules and rituals, other community-building activities can include the development of a class pledge, a class quilt, or a class banner, which serve as visible reminders of the classroom community. All of these activities help to create a climate that can support all of the children and provide clues for appropriate social interactions in the future. A positive classroom climate that supports children is one that models appropriate interactions, maintains routines, minimizes downtime in the schedule of the day, and scaffolds each child's behavior as a community member. Another support for children living in the social world of school is the creation of routines. Routines ensure predictability and security for children.

Routines and Schedules

Routines are important because they help us mange change. Like most of us, children handle change best if it is expected and if it happens in the context of a known routine. A routine is something you do on a regular basis. It is a fixed program. For example, before you eat, you always wash your hands. Or, before you start the car, you always buckle your seat belt and adjust the mirrors. These routines are predictable and can even promote a feeling of mastery in managing life's challenges. Over time, these successes can lead to handling the successful management of bigger tasks and challenges. Routines and schedules help the community of parents and children understand what will happen and how events are organized during the school day. Having a routine and a schedule provides predictability and assurance for the child, thus promoting a feeling of security for children and their families.

A schedule is a list of planned activities or things to be done. Usually a schedule has dates and times associated with it. For example, your schedule might show that you always go to the library at 1:00 p.m. on Wednesdays and to lunch at noon every day. In planning the schedule, the details will depend upon the age of the children, the length of the day, and the curricular goals. Once the schedule is established, posting it assists children in knowing what to do next and assures predictability of the day. Thus, the schedule reassures and provides a stable social situation as children learn.

Tricky times of change for children in your care are arrivals, transitions, and dismissal. The development of routines for these situations will assist in developing children's ability to predict and understand the behavioral goals for social behavior. Variables to consider are whether the children arrive all at once, gradually, with their families, on the bus, or walking. You will need to decide routines for welcoming children and entering the classroom. You will also need to develop a routine for what the children do every day when they enter the classroom. For example, can the children talk and share or must they go to their table or a carpet? As you think about these variables, you will want to minimize wait time for children, especially during transitions. Consider the use of line games such as, "I am thinking of someone who has a blue shirt on" or "What do I have on that is shiny?" These games can keep children occupied and engaged during a transition time as well as promote learning.

There are many clues you can give to children to signal when a routine will start. These signals alert the children to the fact that a change is going to happen. Besides verbal cues, you can develop hand signals and other visual cues such as flicking a light switch off and on or putting on a special cap to indicate transitions and gather attention. For example, Ms. Garcia always plays a certain tune on a xylophone as an indication that cleanup time is beginning. This alerts the children to the transition and helps them prepare for it both physically and emotionally.

Besides transitions, one of the more difficult times for children is when the teacher is working with a small group of children and the other children are supposed to be working alone. As the teacher, you know this is a difficult situation for the children in your classroom to manage, so you decide to develop a routine for the children to ask for help when you are busy with others. Together with the children, you decide on the following routine for asking for your assistance when you are busy: First, the children are to ask a friend for help and see if they can get their question answered or problem solved. If not, the next step is to check the wall to see if the answer is on a poster or a display, and finally, if neither of these work, they are to tap the teacher's shoulder or leg two times to signal that assistance is needed. You can assure the children that the two-tap signal will be responded to in a timely fashion. Planning these elements of the schedule and the flow of the day will leave time to support those children who may require more assistance to follow rules, rituals, and routines. When children understand and know the routine, they will follow it and appreciate the security of its predictability. Then, when someone needs assistance in learning the routine, you can provide a cue, a variation, or a suggestion to maintain the cohesion of the community.

One approach for assisting teachers in thinking about routines is the SECURe (Bailey et al., 2012). This approach assists teachers in thinking about routines that they may take for granted. Instead of merely saying to a group of 4-year-olds, "It's time to go to centers," structure support for children with visual cues such as a chart with all of the centers listed and the number of seats available. Children can then pick up their name cards and place them in a chart pocket or magnetic board to indicate where they will go. They can then move their card when they change centers. This frees you to help children who may have difficulty making a choice and creates order in a transition time. In the primary grades, if you require the children to write headings on papers, make sure to provide a model and practice so that it becomes routinized for the children. There are many other times throughout the day when you will need to develop routines. Some examples are turning in papers, working alone, working with a friend, and taking a bathroom break. Setting routines for each of these situations promotes order and predictability.

You will want to develop routines for yourself as well. For example, what routine will you use for grouping for instruction? Often we think of grouping children by ability or achievement level, but you will want to try to vary the groups so that the children have an opportunity to work with a variety of classmates. This permits opportunities for children to form friendships with all of the children, as well as learning opportunities.

All of these decisions you must make about rules and routines are actually an approach to thinking about supporting, elaborating, and developing child behavior for successful social skills. This approach is known as *developmentally appropriate guidance*. Using developmentally appropriate guidance will contribute to the overall classroom environment and will help you in creating the environment you want for the children in your classroom.

Developmentally Appropriate Guidance

There are many terms used to describe the ways in which adults and children interact. In early childhood classrooms, one of the main responsibilities of a teacher is to mentor and guide children for social success at school and in the community. The choices that you use to facilitate children's understanding of the social life of the classroom are reflected in the terms that are used to describe the personal interactions you have with the children. In education, we often use the term *manage*, which suggests an external adult determination of goals for classroom functioning. This concept is related to the idea that the adult must be responsible for the organization of learning and the basic safety of the children. Another term that is frequently used is *discipline*. Discipline often suggests punishment for wrongdoing. Most early childhood educators eschew the punishment approach to regulating interactions with children, and instead try to help children through teaching social skills, and through the creation of expectations and the use of natural and logical consequences. Gartrell (2004) describes an approach to facilitating child understanding of the social life of the classroom that characterizes the teacher's role as one who provides guidance as opposed to discipline. Gartrell (2004) describes *guidance* as developmentally appropriate, culturally responsive education in order to reduce the occurrence of classroom problems. Through guidance, the teacher creates a positive learning environment for each child in the group (Gartrell, 2004). This use of the term *guidance* was adopted by NAEYC in its discussion of developmentally appropriate practice (Bredekamp, 1987, Copple & Bredekamp, 2009) and, to date, *guidance* continues to have a broad definition that includes guiding children in making decisions and recognizing that children's conflicts and "misbehavior" are important learning opportunities. Guidance requires that the teacher listen carefully to what children say, model problem solving, and give patient reminders of rules (Copple & Bredekamp, 2009, pp. 35–36).

In the broadest sense, guidance, as described by developmentally appropriate practice, implies the teachers' role as the humane "sage on the side," providing assistance to children as they learn to navigate the social world of school and child care settings. As outlined by Gartrell (2004), guidance teaches democratic life skills wherein teachers use non-compliance with rules and routines as teaching opportunities. It is the teacher's responsibility to try to understand the child's behavior. The teacher builds a learning community for all learners (Gartrell, 2004, p. 176). In contrast, teacher-child interaction viewed from a behavioral perspective focuses more on the behavior of individuals and encourages the notion of self-responsibility. One aspect of this view is taking into account the development of children's capacity to regulate their behavior and assume responsibility for consequences of behavioral actions. Of course, the child's capacity to regulate personal behavior in social situations is developmental and evolving, and it can be supported with intentional teaching. This view assumes that the teacher has a role in the development of the child's executive functioning.

Executive Function

Most children will eventually develop the capacity to self-regulate; however, there will be individual variation in each child's trajectory toward the capacity to control impulses, to begin and sustain tasks, and to plan and organize actions in social situations. Usually, it is those children who have difficulty in establishing self-control whose behavior will require intervention and support from you. In his book on executive function, Kaufman (2010) describes seven strategies to make classrooms friendly for children with executive functioning challenges. He emphasizes and illustrates ways for teachers to: 1) provide individualized support and monitoring when children are expected to work by themselves on tasks; 2) provide explicit step-by-step directions and modeling of the steps for new rules, tasks, or materials, and leave infographic or verbal charts available as cues; 3) make the translations to real life explicit, such as ways to play with friends at home or in the park, based on rehearsed class strategies; 4) modify the task required for success, such as drawing a picture to represent the story rather than writing a paragraph; 5) offer many opportunities to practice rules, assignments, and activities with oral, visual reminders as scaffolding support; 6) maintain clear and consistent rules and routines, with advance rehearsal of any changes for activities such as whole-school assemblies; and 7) as you plan, identify situations and tasks that may be difficult for particular children and provide oral or visual steps to support success. Some of the social-emotional skills to teach include following rules, engaging in routines, following directions, identifying feelings in oneself and others, controlling anger and impulses, sharing materials, taking turns, giving compliments, being generous, being helpful, negotiating, problem solving, apologizing when appropriate, expressing empathy with others, and learning how to calm down. When teaching social skills to a class or an individual, you will want to demonstrate the skill, watch the children's progress, give opportunities to use the new skill, and provide opportunities to generalize the new social skill. Some ways to teach social skills include direct teaching, modeling, peer practice, singing, prompts, and games (Fox & Lentini, 2006).

Cues that a teacher may offer to help children include asking them what they want to accomplish in a specific situation, asking what they are doing in that situation, and then helping them to evaluate whether what they are currently doing matches their goals. If what they are doing is not helping to meet their goals, children are asked to create a plan for improvement. This technique is outlined in Wubbolding's (2011) adaptation of William Glasser's Reality Therapy theory for individual counseling in the classroom, using what he calls the **WDEP** (What, Do, Evaluate, Plan) framework. For example, you look around your classroom and see that Ruby is throwing paper balls at the waste basket. Using the **WDEP** method, you ask Ruby, "What is your goal right now?" Ruby responds, "I am supposed to be finishing writing a story about my favorite food." You respond to Ruby, "Well, what are you actually doing right now?" and Ruby states, "I am making paper balls and throwing them." You then ask Ruby if this activity matches her goal of finishing her story. When she responds that it does not, you ask her how she can change her behavior to meet her goal and ask her what help she needs from you, the teacher, to accomplish this. The WDEP technique is helpful for redirecting children without exerting adult superiority, punishment, or blame.

Another technique is outlined in the SECURe program (Bailey et al., 2012). Using the SECURe technique, teachers develop a stop-and-think signal for children, such as holding up a hand and pointing to their head. This cues the child that they may wish to think about whether they wish to continue talking with Daniel when Daniel is trying to read a book. Another cue is a teacher modeling the use of binoculars to cue children to "put on their binoculars" to demonstrate a need to focus on what will happen next. The possibilities of what to use for cues and props are endless and can include items such as puppets, hats (to signify putting on a thinking cap), songs, rhymes, pictures, and so on. Another popular cue is the 3-inch rule, i.e., the distance of a hand from another child's head. This rule communicates soft talking when groups are working quietly at their seats, so that Ahmed knows if he wants to ask Aidenn a question, his voice should meet the 3-inch criteria in terms of volume. Each of these cues and approaches can be used within a classroom setting and can be developed by individual teachers with support from specialists and families when serving children with challenging behavior. However, there is a growing trend to develop school-wide approaches to promoting child development and social success for all children in an inclusive environment. This school-wide approach is called Positive Behavioral Intervention and Supports (PBIS).

PBIS and Bullying

One approach to helping schools and teachers maintain a humanistic respectful classroom and schoolwide climate is for teachers to use the following framework of beliefs for support: 1) children learn how to behave and they can change their approaches for varying situations, particularly if there is a conflict with established routines and rules; 2) helping children change will require study of the situation that triggers challenging responses; 3) planned interventions emphasize scaffolding for prevention and learning new behaviors with instruction; 4) support is personal for individuals and valued by the classroom community; 5) for extreme challenges, teamwork with mental health experts is required (Causton & Tracy-Bronson, 2015, p. 138). This approach provides a framework that sets up the expectation that children want to and can be a part of a caring and successful school community and that the adults in the community can and will work together to help any child who is having problems with successful engagement in the community. For example, one of the special situations encountered within a classroom or within a school is bullying. There are five types of bullying: 1) physical aggression, such as hitting, slapping, tripping, and pushing; 2) verbal bullying, such as calling names, taunting, and threatening; 3) social-emotional bullying, such as exclusion, withdrawing attention, gossip, rumor, and rejection of friendship overtures; 4) destruction of property, such as intentionally breaking a favored toy, tearing up pictures drawn, marking a coat with permanent marker, etc.; and 5) cyber bullying, such as posting rumors or embarrassing pictures on social media, sending texts, or e-mails. "Among school-aged children, bullying is characterized by: (1) aggressive behavior; (2) that is repeated, or has the potential to be repeated; and (3) that reflects an imbalance of power between the aggressor and the victim (Gladden, Vivolo-Kantor, Hamburger, & Lumpkin, 2014). Forms of bullying can be categorized as "direct," which includes physical attacks, threats, theft, and name-calling, or "indirect," which includes gossip, lying, and exclusion (Crick, Casas, & Ku, 1999). There are also established roles in bullying interactions: bullies, victims, bystanders, and bullies who are also victims themselves (bully-victims) (Alsaker and Gutzwiller-Helfenfinger, 2010; Sullivan, 2011; Levine & Tamburrino, 2014). Some victims have also been described as "aggressive victims" in that their behavior may provoke peer victimization, and when provoked, they retaliate with exaggerated hostility (Olweus, 2001). Existing research articulates that a young child's aggressive behaviors become more organized into bullying in preschool (DeVooght et al., 2015, p. 3). Therefore, as teachers we must be vigilant in identifying bullying situations within the school community, for the bully often coerces the bullied to be quiet. Intervention by teachers and families is required to support the change of behavior for the bully and the bullied. Awareness of human rights and the teaching of social skills are important ways to mitigate the potential impact of such behaviors. The support of routines, rules, and classroom climate that is based on respect also mitigates the potential development of bullying.

Successful Teaching

As teachers, we must pay attention to the elements of success so that we may be proud of ourselves as facilitators of child growth and learning and most importantly of the children who work to meet the intended academic and social outcomes that we have worked so hard to achieve. The elements of successful teaching represent a complex set of interacting expectations that are described as having appropriate expectations for each child's learning profile, recognition of children's social needs in a positive learning environment, using the time for activities effectively, making the pace of instruction differentiated for all learners, creating active learning activities, encouraging conceptual understanding as well as ways to apply learning, helping children manage their time toward completion of projects and activities, creating clear expectations, having enthusiasm for the lessons, creating warm relationships with students and families, pacing the material deliberately, teaching for mastery of skills and concepts, giving feedback and review as needed, and finally, possessing the underlying subject matter knowledge to support the curriculum (Lavigne & Good, 2013).

Children describe effective teachers as those who take time with them, enjoy being in the class, ask questions to help them discover the answer, have a sense of humor, are patient and understanding, are willing to learn about them and their culture and those who inspire and push them. This type of teacher is called the *warm demander,* and the term is also used to describe successful teachers of African American children. The warm demander is a teacher who believes in children and who does not give up on teaching them (Delpit, 2012, pp. 76–77). This type of effective teaching also meets the definition of the culturally relevant teacher.

Cultural Relevance

Culture is a socially created construct and is influenced by historical events, politics, economics, and other social constructs. Our public schools have become increasingly diverse. In 2014, for the first time in our nation's history, the number of Asian, Latino, and African American children surpassed the number of non-Hispanic White children. This diversity means that most of our nation's teachers must be prepared to teach children from cultures that are different from their own. *Culturally relevant teaching* is a term that was introduced by Gloria Ladson-Billings (1992) when she described a teaching pedagogy that

FIGURE 2.7 Multiethnic classroom of children eating.
Source: iStock

empowers students intellectually as well as socially, emotionally, and politically. In her 1994 book *The Dreamkeepers: Successful teaching for African-American students*, she states that the culturally relevant teacher does this by using referents to teach children skills and to impart knowledge (Ladson-Billings, 1994). As culturally relevant teachers, our job is to create a bridge between the child's home and school life. To do this we must help each child identify with and maintain their home culture and language. We must accommodate our teaching to their cultural beliefs and customs, and promote the values, beliefs, histories, stories, and traditions of the children and families we serve (Nieto, pp. 99–100). In addition,

> Culturally relevant teaching uses student culture in order to maintain it and to transcend the negative effects of the dominant culture. Negative effects are brought about in multiple ways in the classroom. For example, many of the children in our classrooms do not see their own history, culture, or background represented in the textbooks or curriculum we use to teach them. Often times, when they do, they see their history, culture, or background distorted.
>
> (Ladson-Billings, 2009, p. 19)

Remember when you were presented with the second grade classroom that was engaging in a study unit on Japan? The items being used in that curricular unit were not only inappropriate, but they were also distorted and uninformed. The teacher who was teaching that unit was not using culturally relevant curricular items.

The cross-cultural zone is the social space where students and teachers of different cultures meet and contend with one another. In the cross-cultural zone—which exists in our classrooms across the nation—teachers and children grapple with identity development, acculturation, acculturation stress, cultural privilege, historical mistrust, historical guilt, fear, anger, learning, and curiosity. "The ability to negotiate the dynamic in the cross-cultural zone can make or break relationships and hinder or help learning" (Saifer et al., 2011, p. 10).

As we seek to understand the cultures of the families and children we work with, we need to be mindful that around the world the role and status of children, gender, and the way children are enculturated and disciplined, as well as tolerance for misbehavior, will provide opportunities for teachers and families to negotiate in the best interests of the child. "Culturally responsive educators attempt to negotiate the cultural conflict that their positions of power often represent" (Cooper, Jewell, He, & Lewin, 2011, p. 158).

In conclusion, as a culturally competent teacher you will strive to establish developmentally appropriate teaching and learning processes that are based on democratic principles, educational equity, human rights, and social justice (Gallavan, 2010, p. 13). You will want to include the children in the development of meaningful activities as well as in rule setting and making decisions. You must strive for educational equity, in which all of the children and families in your classroom are provided information, access, and opportunity for success. All of the children and families should have the necessary tools, equipment, and materials to learn and achieve. Their home languages should be used for communication purposes when possible and their languages, customs, and cultures should be treated with respect and dignity.

Summing It Up

There is much to think about in setting up your classroom for successful learning and social interaction. A well-thought-out and well-designed physical space, as well as a stable and orderly environment, provide security for learners. While there are a multitude of ways to arrange and order your space, make sure that there is some of "you" in the space and that it meets the needs of the children and families you are serving. The kinds of materials you choose, and the rules, routines, and schedule that you design (often times with the children's assistance and input), can help to empower children for decision making and structured interactions with peers. Look back at the sketches and lists you made while reading this chapter and keep them in a safe place: You will pull them out again when you have your new classroom. Think of them as dynamic creations that you can add to and change over time as you design, work on, and rethink your classroom. Finally, strive to become a culturally relevant teacher who provides developmentally appropriate guidance and support to all of the children and families that you serve.

Chapter 2 Activities

1. You have just been assigned to your new classroom and have been given a class list with the names of each of the children in your care. You are very excited about setting up your room and want everything to be perfect for the first day of school. You eagerly set about decorating your room and hang posters, letter and number charts, sight-word posters, and other colorful posters high up on your walls so that they will not get destroyed by eager hands.

    In addition to decorating the walls, you create workstations for various curricular areas such as science and math, including small manipulatives and blocks, for example. You have decided that the children will get to choose whatever they want to do each day and you will let them just go to that area after your initial circle time. Your circle time rug is in the back of the classroom, tucked away in a corner so that it is not visible from the front of the room.

    Based on your decisions on the room setup, can you list at least three issues that you might confront when the children arrive on the first day? Reflect upon your answers using the best-practice ideas discussed in the chapter.

2. In addition to setting up your physical space, you also think quite a bit about your classroom rules. You eagerly set about creating a list of rules for the children to see on their first day. You have listed six rules that state:

    1. No running in the classroom.
    2. No talking out of turn.
    3. Do not hit others.
    4. No yelling in the school building.
    5. No tattletales allowed.
    6. Do not bring toys from home.

    You hang the rules at the front of the room and also put a poster listing them on the door to your classroom so that the children see it when they come into the classroom.

    1. How might you have gone about developing class rules after the children are in the classroom with you?

2. Can you rewrite each of the class rules to be restated in a positive rather than a negative tone?
3. Do you think six rules is an appropriate number for a group of 4-year-olds? 7-year-olds? Explain.

3. Simone is an active and verbal child. During outdoor play you notice that the other girls tend to do as she demands. One day, while you are observing the children during their play outside, you overhear Simone telling Keely and Ginger to tell Cee Cee that she cannot play with them because she is too fat. Keely and Ginger eagerly take their task to heart and when Cee Cee tries to join their game of tag, Keely and Ginger run away, screaming "No, Cee Cee, you can't play with us. You are too fat to play." Cee Cee looks dejected for a moment and then ignores them and starts running in their direction to join the game anyway. Simone then runs toward Keely and Ginger and starts yelling "Go away, Cee Cee, you can't play today." Keely and Ginger join her and soon all three girls are yelling and giggling, "Go away, Cee Cee, you can't play today."

How might you handle this situation in a developmentally appropriate way? What can you say to the girls, and what actions can you take if they are 4 years old? Would you react differently to a group of 6–7-year-old girls?

3

Implementing Effective Curriculum
Dom Gullo

In this chapter, I explore ways to implement effective curricula. As teachers, we are responsible for using standards, benchmarks, and expected outcomes for the children we teach. When we are implementing developmentally appropriate practice, we seek rich content. We implement themes, and we require curricula using intentional teaching and a broad array of child discovery activities. All of this work is paired with assessment strategies to document child progress. Effective implementation of curriculum requires the use of differentiated strategies and accommodations for all of our learners. These are the topics explored in this chapter.

Implementing Developmental Appropriate Practice

As early childhood educators, we shape curricular content and structure, and we advocate for positioning child development at the forefront of our thinking when promoting the best ways to accomplish learning and development goals. At the very heart of developmentally appropriate practice is the recognition that children are individuals, each with a unique developmental path. This means that we may see erratic development, splintered development, and disparities across learning and developmental domains.

For children who present challenging behaviors, we must seek to understand their developmental trajectories and special behavioral needs. This is tantamount to supporting their academic progress. One of the areas for support and individualization that is most critical for overall learning success is the conscientious teaching of social-emotional skills. For all children in the early years, teaching and providing opportunities to practice social skills should be an integral element of the curriculum. These teaching and learning opportunities provide children with the personal resources and relationship skills they need in order to benefit from and emotionally connect to positive classroom environments. Children with challenging behaviors will need individualized approaches to instruction in order to benefit from the social-emotional learning aspects of curriculum. The strategies used to teach social-emotional learning skills are embedded within an overall philosophy of teaching, learning, and curriculum development.

Connections Between Curriculum and Strategies

Children learn in various ways and through various means. The ways children learn can be described as induction, cognitive dissonance,

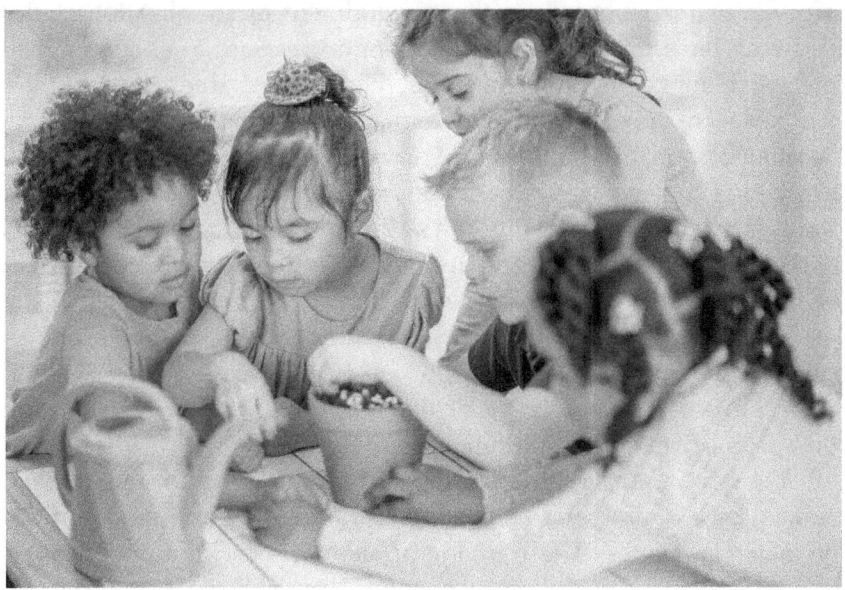

FIGURE 3.1 Children learning by doing.

Source: iStock

physical exploration, and social interaction. Using induction, children compare new knowledge to past experiences to see differences and similarities, thus expanding personal knowledge. Cognitive dissonance is the process children use to try to fit new ideas into what they already know. Children gain physical knowledge by exploring objects and activities through the process of engaging their fine and gross motor skills. Children also learn through social interaction with peers, teachers, family, and community members who are part of their world. In addition, children learn through the sociodramatic construction of play and play writing. These are five of seven ways that children learn as described by Fromberg (2012). Taking these into account, we must be sure that curriculum development and implementation connect to all of the ways that children learn.

One important way to be an effective teacher and implementer of learning experiences is to ensure that you know your students. Whether it's at the beginning of the year, when a new student enters the program, it is imperative that you assess the prior knowledge and experiences that young children bring to school. What have their learning experiences been? Are they kindergarteners with years of child care under their belt? Did they experience a drill-and-practice program, or a program that focused on the development of socialization skills? Did they have no prior formal learning experience at all? Is English their first language? Have they missed half of first grade because their families were moving from place to place? Or have they missed school because of catastrophic illness? Each of these variables plays a role in shaping the knowledge base that children bring to school. Each of these variables will affect children's ability to adapt to the expectations of the school environment and determine the degree to which they will benefit from the learning experiences that are prepared for them.

Part of really knowing the children in your classroom is understanding their cultural backgrounds. In this way, you demonstrate that you possess knowledge of the traditions, values, and cultural understandings of the children and families you serve. Your program will then meet four important anti-bias program goals to support each child's self-awareness of personal cultural identity and the identities of their classmates. The four important goals include appreciating family traditions, modeling respect for all members of the program community, using the primary languages of the children you serve, and recognizing the progress of children who are English learners as they develop fluency in English. If you value family traditions, you will promote child confidence and family pride, which will stand children in good stead for creating a positive social identity. Your program will support young children's capacity to interact with others when you model and reinforce respect for and appreciation for cultural and personal diversity. When possible, using the child's primary language demonstrates the value that you place on various communication approaches in fostering relationships. By the same token, you will show caring relationships with children when you value their ways of communicating and progress in their efforts towards learning English. By involving children in developing rules for the classroom and in managing personal conflict for themselves, you will help children recognize unfair practices in our classrooms, schools, playgrounds, and communities. The involvement of children in conflict management provides opportunities for them to learn the vocabulary related to self-efficacy and unfair practices. Your classroom can serve as a laboratory for young children to recognize bias, so you need to identify ways to confront bias through learned behavioral strategies and various curricular experiences, including children's books (Derman-Sparks & Edwards, 2010, p. xiv). A program with these foundational cultural understandings will use a curricular approach that is culturally relevant:

> Culturally relevant teaching uses student culture in order to maintain it and to transcend the negative effects of the dominant culture. The negative effects are brought about, for example, by not seeing one's history, culture, or background represented in the textbook or curriculum or by seeing that history, culture, or background distorted.
> (Ladson-Billings, 1995, p. 19)

As a teacher of young children, you are the first "school person" to demonstrate respect for the diversity of your students and teach them to be understanding of each other. All of the curriculum content and teaching strategies that you use must firmly address the complex and dynamic nature of culture. During the process of learning to understand the children and families in your care, you will also learn how to adapt your curriculum content and teaching strategies appropriately. Besides practicing culturally relevant teaching, another undergirding philosophy to anchor your approach to teaching is universal design for learning.

Universal Design for Learning

The universal design for learning approach to curricular development is described as one that gives everyone a chance to learn. This approach "provides a blueprint for creating instructional goals, methods, materials, and assessments that work for everyone—not a single, one-size-fits-all solution but rather flexible approaches that can be customized and adjusted for individual needs" (National Center for Universal Design, 2016). There are three principles of universal design for learning: present learning from multiple perspectives, allow learners to express comprehension in various ways, and provide learning activities that permit multiple ways to engage. So, first and foremost think about multiple means of representing curriculum and strategies. That is, how will children see and hear the planned teaching? What language, expressions, and symbols will be used? How will comprehension be measured?

A second principle requires teachers to think about multiple means of expression for curricular outcomes. What physical actions

FIGURE 3.2 Universal design environment to serve all learners.
Source: iStock

demonstrate comprehension? How will the learner show expressions and communication? Which executive function skills will be included and supported?

The third principle requires that multiple means of engagement are provided. How will you interest the learner? How will you sustain effort and persistence? What will you do to support self-regulation in the classroom setting (Blackhurst et al., 1999, CAST)? These principles guide the development of differentiated instruction for all learners in an inclusive environment. Thus, regardless of the curricular approach that you utilize, you can customize instruction for each learner by recognizing the universal design principles, which leads you to the development of differentiated instruction.

Differentiated Instruction

Differentiated instruction means that instead of thinking about children in your classes as 4-year-olds or 6-year-olds, and planning curriculum experiences for these children based solely on their chronological age, you will plan for Wei Wei, Ahmad, Jean, LeShawn, and Joey as individuals. Each child is unique and comes with their own individual language, cognitive, social, and emotional needs. Each child brings to the classroom experiences that reflect their own distinct cultural background. As their teacher, you will differentiate the content of your curriculum, as well as instructional and implementation strategies, to ensure that each member of your class can be a self-empowered successful learner, reaching their optimal potential. You will modify the physical, social, and temporal environment to promote engagement and learning; modify materials so children can participate as independently as possible; appropriately modify learning tasks to promote success for each learner; adjust the curriculum for each child's interest; obtain and use special equipment for particular individual needs; and provide opportunities for children to support each other's learning through small group activities and buddy interactions. Differentiated instruction promotes full citizenship in the classroom for all children and demonstrates commitment to the belief in children's ability to think; belief in the individuality of children; belief in the reciprocity of peer and teacher relationships; and belief that the classroom is a shared space for all learners to enjoy and be accomplished in their learning endeavors (Rapp, 2015). These tenets are true whether you are making day-to-day curriculum decisions or long-range curricular plans.

Classroom Example

Miss Jeanne teaches twenty-five 5- and 6-year-olds in a public school setting with the support of a teaching assistant. Careful observation and listening give Miss J. effective information to know each student in depth in order to successfully differentiate curriculum content and implementation strategies. She acknowledges that there are some developmental and cultural similarities among the children in her class; she spends much time at the beginning of the school year getting to know and appreciate the uniqueness that each child contributes to the classroom community. Ongoing procedures such as circle time at the start of each day create meaningful connections for the children as they share familiar songs and nursery rhymes, excitedly chatter about what they did the previous evening, and talk about what they will learn today. Miss J. knows that differentiated learning and teaching is critical to accommodate for the individuals among her children. She deliberately adjusts instructional strategies, materials, experiences, and activities to guide and facilitate children's learning and development in purposeful ways that account for the differences among them. Miss J. recognizes the significance of choice and decision making for the children in her class. She judiciously structures learning activities and materials in ways that ensure that all children can meet with some success regardless of their developmental status. She encourages children to choose from among the activities and materials that she provides. Miss J. uses active and hands-on learning as an occasion for children to construct their own knowledge. She incorporates a variety of learning contexts into her classroom. She structures the activities so that there is a balance of both child-initiated and teacher-directed activities. The classroom offers the children structure and predictability in environmental and temporal organization. Students come to trust the consistency and regularity of their classroom routine as well as Miss J.'s high expectations for learning. Miss J. provides her students with a safe learning environment that encourages exploration, initiative, positive peer interaction, and cognitive challenge. Materials are chosen that are challenging yet accommodate the wide skill levels represented by the children in the class. Diverse work areas are present in the classroom that are suitable for a wide variety of purposes and learning styles; interaction, collaboration, and cooperative learning; silent reading and/or individual work; project-based learning; writing and listening activities; playing math or language games; and exploring science.

Summary

Developmentally appropriate practice principles, culturally relevant teaching requirements, universal design for learning principles, and the practice of differentiating instruction emphasize the importance of considering the young children we teach as individuals with unique development and learning trajectories, unique experiential backgrounds, and unique interests. We are often children's first teachers, helping them make the transition to the world of school. This often brings into focus the people part of teaching, respecting children in their family settings, and assisting them in the development and achievement of social-emotional learning and academic outcomes. All of these principles and best practice models can be incorporated in the various ways that early childhood teachers create and implement curriculum.

"The curriculum consists of the knowledge, skills, abilities, and understandings children are expected to acquire and the plans for the learning experiences through which those gains will occur. Implementing a curriculum always yields outcomes of some kind" (Copple & Bredekamp,

FIGURE 3.3 The elements of universal design.
Source: iStock

2009, p. 20). This statement elucidates the *NAEYC Position Statement on Developmentally Appropriate Practice in Early Childhood Programs Serving Children from Birth Through Age 8* (NAEYC, 2009) by the leading professional organization for early education. This position advocates for and articulates a constructivist approach to curriculum development. At the heart of a constructivist approach is learning and teaching that are developed by individuals within a particular classroom community.

Constructivist Early Childhood Curriculum

The principles of a constructivist curriculum suggest that teachers of young children need to:

- establish a cooperative socio-moral atmosphere;
- plan to appeal to children's interests;
- teach in terms of the kind of knowledge involved (i.e., physical knowledge, logico-mathematical knowledge, arbitrary conventional knowledge);
- choose content that challenges children; and
- promote children's reasoning using questions in order to:
  - understand each child's thinking;
  - propose things for children to think about;
  - learn the child's behavioral purposes;
  - focus each child's thinking, and model higher order thinking;
  - provide adequate time for children's investigation and in-depth engagement in learning activities; and
  - link teaching to ongoing documentation and assessment of learning.

(DeVries, Zan, Hildebrandt, Edmiaston, & Sales, 2002, pp. 35–51)

This approach to teaching employs various instructional strategies. In particular, instructional strategies that fit well with this orientation to curriculum development are

> intentional, use data-based decision making, are individualized, built on child strengths, preferences and interests, align with family beliefs and values; address target skills and behaviors that are

priorities for the family; address pivotal skills and behaviors that help to make the child more independent and are implemented with high fidelity to the child's particular learning needs.
(Schwartz & Woods, 2015, pp. 78–85)

Teaching in this manner and adhering to the tenets of developmentally appropriate practice recognizes "four phases of the learning process: acquisition of a skill, fluency or ability to use the skill, maintenance of the skill by providing opportunities for practice and generalization of the skill to other social or content situations" (Schwartz & Woods, 2015, p. 77).

Teaching and Learning from a Constructivist Approach

The constructivist approach to teaching and learning supports the belief that knowledge and behavior are constructed; learning occurs as learners are actively involved in the process of making meaning and not merely passive recipients of information. It is critical that a constructivist approach to teaching and learning must still function with content. A key approach to teaching content within the constructivist paradigm that is used in many programs for preschool children, as well as in some K–3 programs, is known as the *thematic approach*.

The use of thematic units provides an integrated approach to teaching and learning, one that incorporates multiple content areas and helps children remain engaged as they draw from multiple skill and knowledge sets. The thematic approach is based, in part, on brain research that challenges the belief that learning and teaching can and should be separated into traditional subject specific domains (Berry & Mindes, 1993). Research by Piaget, Vygotsky, and Bruner support an integrated approach to teaching that cannot be easily separated into traditional academic disciplines. When the same theme occurs across disciplines, children are able to revisit ideas, knowledge, and skills in multiple contexts and apply them in different ways. This results in a much richer understanding of the content that is being learned. Because themes often emerge out of children's interests, this approach to teaching and learning is motivational, builds on children's prior knowledge and understanding, and allows children to demonstrate their understanding in multiple ways and in multiple contexts.

As stated previously, in early childhood preschool and kindergarten programs themes are often drawn from the interests of the children. For example, if a road is closed because the bridge over the river washes out and the commute to school requires a detour, the children who are curious about the ways that water moves, its power, and why the bridge collapses may begin a study of rivers and bridges. Or in the case of the recent floods in Louisiana or the Zika virus in Florida, children may wonder, what causes floods? Where will my family live? Will I ever have toys? What does a mosquito carrying the Zika virus look like? If I live in Idaho, do I have to worry about the Zika virus? As children ask these and other questions, based on what they hear about in the media and family discussions, their teachers will construct a curriculum to give children opportunities to discover answers for themselves and explore the "science" behind the questions and answers in a way that is appropriate for children's level of understanding. Teachers will bring in videos, stories, art materials, and sometimes experts to help the children understand the science and to address their concerns and curiosities implicit in the questions they pose.

In elementary primary grade programs, themes are more likely to be drawn from social studies curricular goals that are established by school district or state program goals, with content often derived from textbooks. However, whether initially driven by child interest or developed to meet required outcomes, "thematic curriculum is an interdisciplinary subject exploration whose components are bound together by a large overarching theme" (Meier, Knoester & D'Andrea, 2015, p. 3). What follows are some examples of curricular themes from actual schools.

Themes at the Mission Hill School in Boston include baking, for the kindergarten class, and the Struggle for Justice—history through the eyes of African Americans—for second and third graders (Meier et al., 2015). Another theme for second and third grade is children as change makers, which focuses on ecology in action (D'Andrea, 2015). For kindergarten children, themes include schoolyard ecology and the endangered turtles of Massachusetts. For a kindergarten class in Brooklyn, New York, Roth and Dinnerstein (2015) describe a study of the wheelchair as a transportation theme. An inclusion class with a child using a wheelchair inspired this investigation. In Salinas, California, Ms. Richman developed a thematic unit on agriculture since so many of the families in the area were involved in the industry (Richman, 2011).

Whether the thematic approach drives the content for a week, a month, or a year depends on the significance of the theme, the age and interests of the learners, and the demands for meeting particular curricular outcome requirements. Many times, the length of the thematic

FIGURE 3.4 Children brainstorming.
Source: iStock

study will depend on how long the children can maintain interest within the thematic context. Thematic studies might also change as a result of changes of interest within a particular unit. For example, a thematic study might start out as a result of interest in how buildings are constructed and "morph" into a study of different types of dwellings.

Another constructivist approach, known as *emergent curriculum*, is widely practiced in preschool programs. "Emergent curriculum refers to the individual interests of students within a classroom that the teacher encourages, allowing time for a student to explore a particular question or topic, providing resources that enrich the curriculum" (Meier et al., 2015, p. 3). Emergent curriculum describes a curriculum that develops from exploring:

- ◆ what is relevant to children;
- ◆ what is interesting to children; and
- ◆ what is personally meaningful to the life experiences of children.

(Jones, 2012)

This approach requires teachers to be knowledgeable of outcome requirements so that children acquire the necessary knowledge, skills, and dispositions that they will need to be successful school learners. Key features of emergent curriculum include the following:

- Emergent curriculum is not linear. It is constantly evolving in response to children's changing needs and interests.
- Emergent curriculum is both flexible and responsive. The curriculum builds on children's changing acquisition of skills and knowledge.
- Emergent curriculum is cyclical. The process of observing children and assessing their progress in order to modify both curriculum and instruction is repeated on a continual basis.
- Emergent curriculum is collaborative. Both teachers and children are part of the decision-making process.
- Emergent curriculum makes children's learning and teachers' teaching visible. Through the process of collaboration, with other teachers, with children, and with families, the process of teaching and learning is documented and reflected upon.

(Stacey, 2008)

One of the best tools for planning when using an emergent curriculum approach is utilizing a graphic organizer that features a web design. This allows you to connect the ideas that occur at the beginning of the topic development, as well as to follow leads that occur as you continue the investigation with children. The web allows you to think about how you will use the children's current language, expand critical thinking, and support academic language development. It will help you see where varied art expressions can come in, suggest materials for children to explore, and promote problem-solving and investigation skills (Jones & Reynolds, 2013).

For example, Figure 3.5 is a web design of a thematic unit on "apples" that might be appropriate for kindergarten or first grade. It depicts the beginning of the organization of the unit, one that was developed by both the teacher and the children in the class. It might have grown out of children bringing apples to school for their lunch or snack, particularly in the fall. The teacher then discusses the topic of apples and brainstorms with the children, asking them what they'd like to learn about apples, often scaffolding their discussion by asking questions or

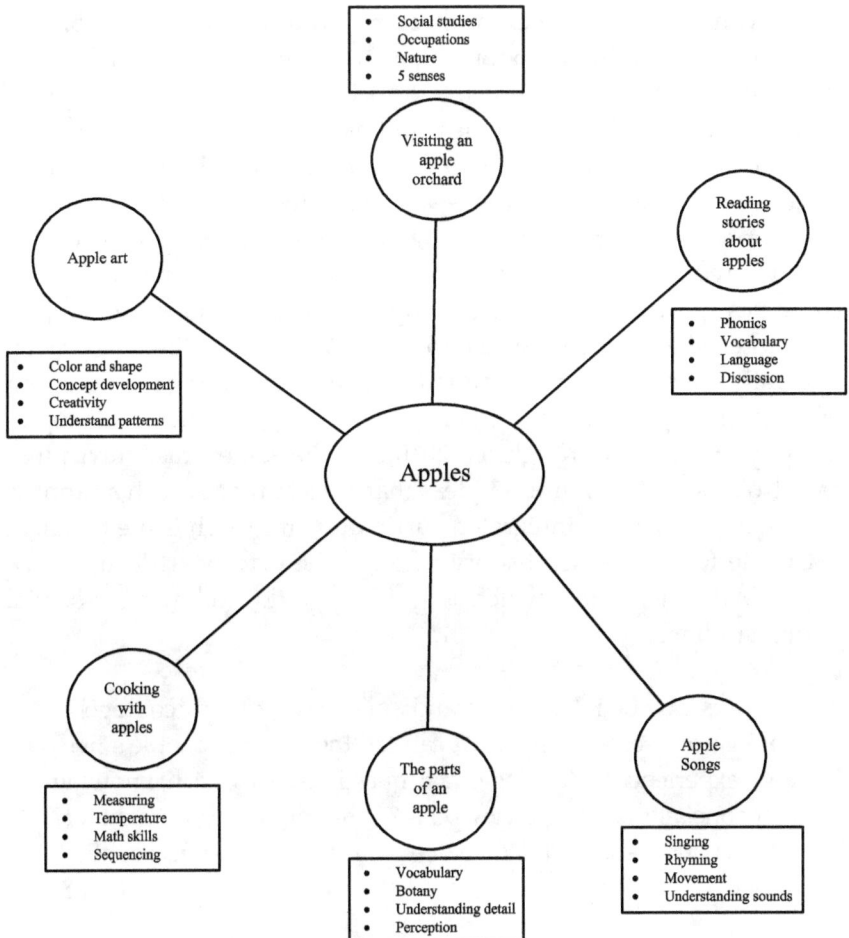

FIGURE 3.5 Apple Theme and Graphic Organizer.

offering suggestions. The web design of the unit is meant to be dynamic in nature, changing as the children's interests change and grow.

When using the emergent curriculum approach and a thematic approach to curriculum development, you can capitalize on the integration of skills and knowledge of various subjects to show children that learning is not about individual subjects, but about the creation of knowledge and skills. "Integrated curriculum is an approach to teaching that weaves disciplinary knowledge from various subjects together to allow students to be at the center of the decision making process" (Meier et al., 2015, p. 3).

As can be seen in the example curriculum web in Figure 3.5, children can have multiple opportunities to learning about numbers, to learn about letters and sounds, and to learn about vocabulary. Each topic can have multiple activities, and each activity can contain multiple subject matter content. With this approach, children can work on projects for long periods of time—as long as their interests are piqued. The emphasis is on problem solving and critical thinking. Curriculum is structured around big ideas. Some topics to think about that demonstrate this approach are the "broad topics such as transportation or grocery store, which can be matched to curricular goals for the year, broken into daily lessons linked to required outcomes, including the collection of children's literature and other media to support the broad topic" (Brophy, Alleman, & Knighton, 2010). At the same time, curriculum can also be structured around ideas that are less broad, such as apples.

An example of an integrated curriculum approach is the theme of "Struggle for justice: US history through the eyes of African Americans" (Williams, 2015), which is guided by the following essential understandings:

> There is power in numbers and solidarity; it takes courage to get justice/create change; Art can tell the story of people's lives and experiences. With essential questions: How can knowing someone's story change viewpoint? What rights do you fight for? When is justice served? When does being different affect equality?
>
> (p. 63)

Williams used songs, photos, and poems to explore the topic of equality, courage, and justice with second and third graders. The integrated curricular approach acknowledges young learners as capable of understanding the complexities of their world. It also models a perspective on thinking about important issues using the skills of various disciplines.

Another constructivist approach to curriculum development is the project approach. While closely related to the thematic approach, there are some fundamental differences.

Project Approach

The project approach is an "in-depth study of a particular topic, usually undertaken by a whole class working on subtopics in small groups, sometimes by a small group of children within a class, and occasionally by an individual child" (Katz, Chard, & Kogan, 2014). Historically, the project approach grew from children's interests, with teachers helping children to elaborate their understandings of their world. This approach is still used in traditional preschool programs. It often begins with a child's curiosity around what's happening around them. For example, suppose the hamburger festival is coming to the neighborhood. In exploration of why such a festival occurs annually, children can learn about what a festival is, why hamburger is important in their community, and expand their thinking to what it takes to run a restaurant, managing staff, budget, food safety, etc. This approach to curriculum emerges from the curiosities of children and requires teachers to connect that curiosity to program goals and to scaffold child understanding through various means. These include, but are not limited to: asking children questions about what they want to know, providing opportunities and materials that will stimulate and further interests, bringing into the class experts in what the children are interested in, and taking excursions outside the classroom and school settings to "where the action is."

The goals of this approach to curriculum development are to keep the content aligned with the children's ideas. There is an inherent need to make the content and activities "doable," and a realization that not all children will be fascinated by a particular topic. Teachers need to work to see how children can be engaged. There should also be recognition of the labor involved in carrying out elaborate themes (Lickey & Powers, 2011). "Additional considerations include the importance of the content, number of children sharing the interest in a particular topic, availability of books and materials to support the endeavor, keeping the content related to program goals" (Lickey & Powers, 2011, p. 103).

When working with required curricular goals and standards, the project approach can be used; however, to be effective, teachers must know the standards and the benchmarks that are expected. As you use a concept web to develop a plan for a project on houses, for example (Helm & Katz, 2010), you map out the big ideas and then connect the link between the required content and skills required.

Another implementation strategy used in project-based learning, described sometimes as *problem-based learning*—a term first used in elementary and high school situations—starts with a teacher-assigned project that fits the curriculum content. In this case, the problem or project is typically assigned to small groups of children working together, rather than a project emerging from the interest of children. This approach allows children the opportunity to participate in the project from multiple interest and skill levels. Elements of this approach to curriculum include the following essential characteristics:

- [using an] anchor to set the stage and generate interest, such as video, narrative, or presentation by the teacher,
- collaboration of the learners,
- driving questions created by the teacher for children to explore,
- child elaboration of the project through questions developed as they investigate,
- opportunities for child reflection,
- feedback by the teacher and project revision ongoing,
- publicly presented project, and finally
- child voice and choice of solutions.

(Bender, 2012, pp. 31–32)

FIGURE 3.6 Children doing a project.
Source: iStock

The critical element of this approach to project-based or problem-based learning is that the question or questions explored are driven from external curricular demands. The philosophy behind the approach is an attempt to make curricular exploration an active experience in critical thinking for children, investigating a big idea generated by the school district or state standards. As described, "Project-based learning is a dynamic approach to teaching in which students explore real-world problems and challenges. With this type of active and engaged learning, students are inspired to obtain a deeper knowledge of the subjects they're studying" (Edutopia, 2016). Whether the question is recycling, food distribution, social justice, or other big ideas, the content and activities used in this approach to curriculum development and implementation can be differentiated for the children in your class and linked to outcome requirements.

Guidelines for conducting project work include:

- encouraging children to test their hypotheses, ideas, and inquiries, thus, building the habit for hypothesis testing;
- encouraging children to converse in small groups and to challenge peers' solutions and thoughts;
- using collaboration processes in both pairs and small groups;
- mixing ages, genders, abilities in small groups;
- encouraging children to share experiences and prior knowledge;
- supporting and allowing children to work on different aspects of a class project;
- guiding the children's reflection process so that the curricular aims are addressed; and
- keeping in mind that hands-on activities give another dimension to children's ability to conceptualize and expand their thinking.

(Essa, Taylor, Pratt, & Roberts, 2012, pp. 28–32)

Problem-based learning and this interpretation of project-based learning are driven from the teacher's perspective, which is usually based on required school or state standards. The approach requires the development of access points for the project so that all learners can accomplish required outcomes. That is, the project should be accessible to children with varying interests, skills, and knowledge. So, for example, suppose Miss Hopkins (the kindergarten teacher) notices that the grass in the nearby park is dead and that soon when the snow comes and melts there will be mud and the potential to fall. She knows that in April the class will observe Earth Day, so she poses the problem for the class: What causes grass in the park to die? The kindergarteners can examine the footprint of the park—that is, where the sidewalks are and how people use the park—which can address geographic standards. Children can examine weather patterns, which will address mathematical content. Some children may address the kinds of grass that are suitable for weather and use, which will address science standards. In this way, children can read, gather data, interpret, illustrate learning, and write up findings. There are in this approach multiple access points for solving this problem-based learning agenda. Of course, Miss Hopkins will link her work to the relevant kindergarten standards for her state. Linking curriculum to outcomes and standards is after all a major responsibility for all teachers in most programs.

Linking Curriculum to Required Outcomes

In all of these various interpretations of the constructivist approach to curricular development, the principles of developmentally appropriate practice can be found. What is required of teachers practicing these iterations of constructivist practice is the careful consideration of required outcomes, the careful observation and data gathering of child progress toward outcomes, and the ability to make bridges for individual child success in the social atmosphere of the classroom community. Foremost, of course, is knowing the children and planning holistically *and* individually, accordingly. While there are programs that apply developmentally appropriate practice based on emergent curriculum without predetermined standards, publicly funded and many corporately funded programs require teachers to document child learning and associate the learning with standards or predetermined goals. However, whether or not conforming to standards is required, best practice suggests that any curricular approach must have developmental targets for children's learning.

One way to keep track of curricular goals and to plan successfully is the Understanding by Design (UbD™) approach developed by McTighe and Wiggins (2012). This is a "planning process and structure to guide curriculum, assessment, and instruction. Its two key ideas are contained in the title: 1) focus on teaching and assessing for understanding and learning transfer, and 2) design curriculum 'backward' from the goals and objectives toward those ends" (McTighe & Wiggins, 2012, p. 1). In this process, curriculum planners and teachers first identify the desired outcomes for a period of time, usually a year; second, they determine what assessment evidence is needed to document learning progress of the children; and third, they plan the learning experiences so that children can acquire the requisite content and skills. Once this approach is used to construct the overall curriculum teaching and learning plan, modifications for individuals are made so each child can be successful.

In most teaching situations, whether in child care settings, preschools, Head Start, or in elementary K–3 grades, when implementing a constructivist approach and UbD, the content of the curriculum should be focused on required programs or standards. For example, recently the *Head Start Early Learning Outcomes Framework: Ages Birth to Five*, with a focus on the continuum of development from infancy, were published (Early Childhood Learning and Knowledge Center [ECLKC] Head Start, 2015). Teachers in Head Start programs will need to adjust their curricular planning in conformance with this framework, which specifies the skills, behaviors, and knowledge that all children in the program must acquire.

The central domains of the Head Start early learning outcomes framework are focused on delineating approaches to teaching and learning in cognition and learning, social-emotional development, language and literacy, and perceptual motor (Early Childhood Learning and Knowledge Center (ECLKC) Head Start, 2015). The framework specifies outcomes by age level for children enrolled in Head Start. Most Head Start centers choose one of the major curriculum models, such as High Scope, which states that the curriculum is "research based and child focused. The High Scope Curriculum uses a carefully designed process—called 'active participatory learning'—to achieve powerful, positive outcome(s)." (High Scope, 2016). Another widely adopted curricular approach is *The Creative Curriculum® for Preschool* (see the Teaching Strategies for Early Childhood website at https:// teachingstrategies.com/solutions/teach/). Both of these approaches to curriculum provide materials that meet the content and outcome requirements of Head Start. The approaches are used in public as well as private schools across the nation. Other well-known models used by Head Start, preschool, and child care centers include Montessori

(American Montessori Society, 2016) and Reggio Emilia (Edwards, Gandini, & Forman, 2012). Once children enter public school programs at age 4 or 5, then state departments of education have learning standards that must be met.

Curriculum and External State Standards

State learning standards are outcome-based by subject area, such as mathematics, English language arts, science, social studies, etc. Most states also have assessment systems that measure aggregated child progress on the standards. Teachers are required to follow and develop curricula that prepare children to meet the standards.

Beginning in 2010, Common Core State Standards (CCSS) developed for the Council of Chief State School Officers were released to provide uniformity of standards across the nation for English language arts and mathematics. Initially, 46 states agreed to the CCSS; the number has fallen to 42 states due to pressure from advocates for state control of standards. In addition to the guidance provided by states for what must be taught, most school districts have independent curricular requirements for each of the elementary grades. The content is designed to ensure that children meet required local and state outcomes, which are usually measured by standardized tests administered at third grade and beyond.

When assessment systems and standards are correlated, this often results in a narrowing of the curriculum, as teachers teach only those areas that will be assessed. In addition to using standards and curriculum documents, teachers are usually also required to use child textbooks for the content in the K–3 grades. Publishers key the content in their texts to national standards and sometimes to the national associations' guidelines and standards for teaching and learning outcomes. Increasingly, child texts and accompanying teacher resources are available online. It might be beneficial to consult these helpful resources for ideas for individualizing instruction. Frequently, textbook publishers also include assessment suggestions so that you can document progress toward meeting school district and state content standards outcome requirements. However, when using these assessment materials and suggestions, make sure that the assessment practices are grounded in best practices for young children, with a strong focus on observing children as they are engaged in the process of learning, documenting children's progress by collecting examples of children's actual classroom work, and collecting evidence from multiple sources of information.

You can find many helpful ideas regarding the assessment of young children's development and learning at the websites of professional associations. Besides the NAEYC (http://naeyc.org), which publishes journals and books geared to the early years, you will also find helpful assessment guidelines and strategies on these professional association websites: International Literacy Association (www.literacyworldwide.org), National Council of Teachers of English (www.ncte.org), National Council for the Teachers of Mathematics (www.nctm.org), National Science Teachers Association (www.nsta.org), and the National Council for Social Studies (www.socialstudies.org). These associations publish journals and have content specifically directed toward grade levels. The International Literacy Association, the National Council of Teachers of English, and the National Council for the Teachers of Mathematics also publish materials that address the CCSS. In addition to these professional associations, there are associations that provide online, books, and journals directed toward special populations of students.

An important resource to support your work with children displaying challenging behavior is the Division for Early Childhood of the Council for Exceptional Children (www.dec-sped.org). This association has a journal with practical suggestions for young children, monographs, books, and a position statement regarding young children with disabilities, including one on challenging behavior. All of these resources can be very helpful in planning to meet the needs of all of the children in your class.

Finally, you need to be aware of associations geared towards children and families from diverse backgrounds and cultures. These resources include: the National Association for Multicultural Association (http://nameorg.org); the National Association for Bilingual Education (www.nabe.org) and Colorin Colorado (www.colorincolorado.org), which is directed toward young dual-language learners. Important national research centers for information on best practices for young children and their families include: Center on the Developing Child at Harvard (http://developingchild.harvard.edu/), Edward Zigler Center in Child Development and Social Policy (http://ziglercenter.yale.edu), Frank Porter Graham Child Development Center (http://fpg.unc.edu), and WestEd (www.wested.org). Each of these centers publishes research results as well as implications for classroom practice for all young children, and especially those with disabilities and dual language learners.

In sum, curriculum planning can benefit from consultation with all of these resources at the beginning of the year, as well as in times when you experience a particular issue with meeting the needs of a child with challenging behavior. In addition to these broad resources, the Technical Assistance Center on Social Emotional Intervention for Young Children (http://challengingbehavior.fmhi.usf.edu) provides examples of practices that can help you in the classroom and in collaborating with families.

Academic Language

Besides thinking about content and teaching strategies as you plan for the year, an important concept related to preparing for today's multicultural classroom is thinking about the ways we help children acquire the vocabulary they need to "speak school." This language is known as *academic language*. This is the language that children need to deepen their understanding of content and to talk with others about the content. It's the language of learning and instruction. This language has specific linguistic features that are related to the particular discipline to which they are associated, including special grammatical constructs and vocabulary. This is the language that teachers must think about as they are developing curricular content and instructional strategies. When planning for instruction, one must ask themselves, "What are the important linguistic features of mathematics? Of social studies? Of English language arts?" (Gottlieb & Ernst-Slavit, 2014). For example, academic language for understanding mathematics includes comprehension of such terms as *odd, even, exchange,* and *grouping,* as well as the names of geometric shapes. For social studies, young learners need to be conversant with terms related to maps, wants and needs, storytelling from the perspective of the past, and including the ideas of community and citizenship. Finally, for English language arts, in addition to the technical ideas of topic sentence, paragraph, and main idea, children come to learn new vocabulary through the discussion of literature. So, as part of instructional planning, teachers are mindful of the peculiar words used for academic work as part of their development as young scholars.

In addition to content-specific language, teachers must also think about the individual needs of children. These will differ according to factors such as whether English is a first or second language, whether the child has language deficiencies in general, and the degree to which they have been exposed to formal academic language in everyday life experiences.

When considering individual differences in teaching young children, it is important that we think about the critical role that social-emotional learning plays in our decision-making process. The teaching of prosocial skills is also an important element in individualizing instruction for young children. As we think about children with challenging behaviors, it is often these skills that must be developed to safeguard success with academics. It goes without saying, however, that all children will require targeted emphasis on social-emotional learning. Part of any curriculum planning should include social-emotional learning as an emphasis. To this end, some state departments of education have developed standards for social-emotional learning while others are in the process of developing social-emotional learning standards (for example, the Collaborative for Academic and Social Emotional Learning, or CASEL, 2016).

Social-Emotional Learning

In today's times, teachers' understanding of children's social-emotional development is not only important background for teachers, but it is also an integral part of the curriculum that focuses on facilitating child development. Focused attention to teaching skills that foster social and emotional development is based on the research that investigates emotional intelligence. Additionally, many states have social-emotional learning standards that must be met. Tangentially related to social-emotional development, federal attention acknowledges the necessity for these standards through character education and anti-bullying education mandates.

CASEL defines social-emotional competence as

> the ability to understand, manage, and express the social and emotional aspects of one's life in ways that enable the successful management of life's tasks such as learning, forming relationships, solving everyday problems, and adapting to the complex demands of growth and development.
>
> (Elias et al., 1997, p. 2)

FIGURE 3.7 Children doing a project together.
Source: iStock

Social-emotional learning includes a number of interrelated elements. First is one's aptitude for emotional self-regulation. Self-regulation is defined as the ability to respond to experiences with appropriate ranges of emotions, either immediate or delayed. Included are:

- Greater capacity to focus and organize thoughts and actions;
- Being more reflective and less impulsive;
- The awareness of and the following of rules pertaining to:
  - deferring gratification;
  - being flexible;
  - realizing that one's thoughts and feelings are separate from others and unique; and
  - being independent and self-motivated.

Second is the capacity to comprehend social norms and customs and behave accordingly. Subsumed here is civic competence: the understanding of what it means to be a community member and the willingness to surrender a portion of one's own individualism for the greater good. A necessary component is the ability to interact with others of diverse backgrounds, diverse from one's own, including gender, race, ethnicity, religion, language and linguistic background, socioeconomic status, and ability/disability.

Third, there is the need to develop the social dispositions and character traits that support the development of social-emotional learning. These include such things as curiosity, humor, and generosity, as opposed to closed-mindedness, argumentativeness, and selfishness (Epstein, 2009, pp. 6–7).

Through classroom attention to personal interactions and community building, teachers can assist children in developing social-emotional competence with the requisite social skills required in schools, community, and at home. Recently, research-based programs that focus on social-emotional development have emerged. One such example is the Pyramid Model (CSEFEL, 2016), which was developed for Head Start, but has wide applicability to all preschool settings. The Pyramid Model suggests that social-emotional learning begins with nurturing and responsive relationships that are facilitated by teachers. High quality supportive environments reinforce young children's learning; targeted social-emotional supports facilitate the development of social-emotional learning. The Pyramid Model is based on a public-health paradigm of promotion, prevention, and intervention. Three levels of mediation are included. The first level supports universal practices for all children in support of their social development. The secondary level of mediation is the prevention level. This includes provisions for targeted supports for those children at risk of challenging behaviors. The tertiary level of mediation is the intervention level. At this level individualized and intensive interventions are provided for the small number of children who exhibit persistent challenges.

Several states have partnered with CSEFEL to provide professional development for both teachers and families. The Technical Assistance Center on Social Emotional Intervention (TACSEI) provides resources that support social and emotional skill development based on the Pyramid Model. For K–3 teachers, suggestions for ways to promote social-emotional learning and guidelines for choosing programs can be found in the CASEL online resources. A guide for early childhood teachers that links best practice to developmentally appropriate practice suggests that teachers:

- pay attention to the development of verbal and non-verbal communication skills,
- foster feelings of self-efficacy in children,

- recognize cultural variations in the ways children express emotion,
- support friendship development with peers,
- foster self-regulation, and
- promote ways of collaborating with peers.
 (Kostelnik, Soderman, Whiren, & Rupiper, 2015)

Additional resources for thinking about social-emotional learning include the Yale Center for Emotional Intelligence (http://ei.yale.edu); Greater Good in Action: Science-Based Practices for a Meaningful Life at University of California, Berkeley (http://ggia.berkeley.edu); and the Social & Emotional Development Lab at the University of California, Davis (http://sedl.faculty.ucdavis.edu).

The curricular implications for social-emotional development and learning link back to the structure that you set up for your classroom community. It is through thinking about the ways that individuals in the room interact as they individually and collectively wrestle with ideas that young children learn and grow in academic settings. A question that needs to be asked is: How do you know that you are successfully implementing the curriculum? Meeting outcome requirements? Facilitating child development? The answers lie in the fact that curriculum effectiveness, teaching effectiveness, and learning progress in children require assessment.

The Dimensions of Assessment

Assessment is a process used to determine the degree to which an individual child possesses a particular attribute (Gullo, 2005). There are three purposes for assessment. First, assessment is used to gain an understanding of a child's development. Second, assessment is used to gain a better understanding of how a child is progressing through a curriculum sequence. Third, assessment is used to determine whether or not a child is potentially at risk for academic difficulties or is in need of special educational services.

Assessment oftentimes begins with purposeful observations of individual children and the group as a whole; that is, what are the players in the room doing? Are they focused on their work? Are they collaborating successfully? Are they engaged? Are they meeting

FIGURE 3.8 Teacher observing children and taking notes.
Source: iStock

outcomes? Observation alone is not sufficient. The observations must be matched against required curricular outcomes and developmental milestones, so that there is documentation of child progress. During the K–3 years, assessment begins to include assessment practices that rely on paper-and-pencil documentation of progress toward outcomes. A good assessment program includes measures from multiple sources, includes information about children from multiple points in time, and is matched to the learning goals. These are important considerations in order to demonstrate that learning goals are being met and that children are progressing developmentally. When there are indications of difficulty, either learning or developmental, then specialized individual assessments are often used.

For children exhibiting challenging behaviors, the specialized method applied after routine intervention has been employed is usually functional behavior assessment (FBA). This formal observational structure utilizes a fine-grain observation and documentation procedure to elucidate exactly why children are exhibiting a particular behavior. The system requires data collection at multiple times before interpretation and intervention are planned. A process for implementation of FBA is as follows:

1. Determine the behavior's function (what does the child accomplish with the behavior?).
2. Chart the occurrence of the behavior (collect information on when and how the challenging behavior is occurring).
3. Design an intervention to meet the child's need (substituting another behavior, and then evaluate whether it is working).

(IRIS Center, 2016)

As an example, Kevin comes to his first-grade class and sits in his assigned seat, but almost every day, it seems to Ms. Lindstrom, a child complains that Kevin trips them. This behavior usually happens when children are working at their seats and Ms. Lindstrom is working with a small group. She asks the school social worker or a colleague to come observe small group time. The observer records what is happening before the tripping and after the tripping. After analyzing the data, kept on a spreadsheet, Ms. Lindstrom and the observer notice that Kevin has usually finished his assigned work and that he trips only boys, and that immediately after the tripping, the boys begin to talk about hockey. So, what is the function of the behavior—gaining social interaction with peers? A solution that might be proposed is for Kevin to be allowed to chat with a peer when he has finished his work for a specified period.

While this example is simplistic, the principles are illustrated. A child is disrupting the class with behavior that can't be tolerated. Why is it happening? What is the perceived gratification for the child? How can you meet his need with a more socially acceptable behavior? To use this assessment technique, it is best to work with a multidisciplinary assessment team, since some interventions may be occurring at home and will require collaboration with families.

Conclusions

Curriculum planning must be a thoughtful practice that is grounded in knowledge of child development as well as an understanding of the particular children within the class. Planning is done on multiple levels. At the macro level, teachers use the tools provided by a program, such as special curricular guides, textbooks, and outcome requirements. At the monthly or weekly levels, teachers hone the details and ultimately decide "what to do on Monday." Within the course of a day, teachers adapt their practice in response to the particular needs of the children as a group or as individuals. For example, a child falls and must go to the nurse, the yard service personnel begin maintenance by operating the lawn mower outside your classroom window, snow starts to fall, or a family member stops by and you must chat immediately. Each situation requires adapting to the day's specific situations and special efforts to reassure the children as well as maintain a comfortable social-emotional atmosphere.

Chapter 3 Activities

1. You are a new first-grade teacher at Munger School. It is August and school begins right after Labor Day. Ms. Eisely, the principal, just mailed the class list to you. In your class of 25 first graders, you will have three children who have IEPs. These children include one with a speech delay, one with a learning disability, and one who is diagnosed with Asperger Syndrome. You are thinking about your reading program and Common Core 1 (CC1): Foundational Skills: Students gain a working knowledge of concepts of print, alphabetic principle, and other basic conventions. (Pennsylvania Department of Education State Academic Standards, www.pdesas.org/Standard/View). Using the principles of universal design for offering multiple means of presenting early literacy content, multiple means of outcomes assessment, and multiple means of engagement, how will you plan to teach all of your students, so they can meet this standard? What will you do the first week of school to assess the entrance skill level of your class? What curricular modifications will you need for the three children with IEPs? How will you use the IEPs to guide your thinking? How will you differentiate instruction while attending to the behavior of the first graders? What challenges do you anticipate?
2. You just moved to Oakland, California and will be teaching kindergarten. You do not know much about Fruitvale, the neighborhood where your school is located. After you

arrive, you learn that the school draws children from under-resourced communities and that the school district recently adopted a strategic plan: Pathway to Excellence. Thinking about culturally relevant pedagogy, how will you learn more about the cultural values of the families where you will be teaching? How do the cultural values compare to your own? What curricular materials will you need so that you can communicate respect for all of the cultures of your kindergarteners? How might you connect your preparation by visiting the local child care centers? When you learn about child-rearing practices and child care rules, how will these factors influence your curriculum and strategies?

3. After reading this chapter and the discussion of project-based learning, you have renewed commitment to the principles of developmentally appropriate practice and constructivist teaching strategies. Your school is worried about the Spring Partnership for Assessment of College and Career Readiness (PARRC) assessment (https://parcc.pearson.com/). The school's mathematics scores declined last year. Many teachers in your school think that direct instruction will make the scores rise. Your school already uses Measuring Academic Progress (MAP) (www.nwea.org/assessments/map/) to regularly provide diagnostic information about child progress throughout the year, so you don't believe that a drill-and-practice approach to teaching mathematics is necessary. Using the principles of UbD and the discussion of the project approach to learning, show how you can meet the third-grade state standards while providing a constructivist approach to learning. Show how the diagnostic information from the MAP assists you in grouping your students for instruction. Look at the PARRC practice items and show how these might be used as models for developing activities in your classroom.

4. Imagine that you are teaching kindergarten and you are notified that you will be receiving a new child in your classroom. The parents have asked to meet with you and during your meeting they inform you that their child Lyssa is in a wheelchair. They tell you that they would like to come and introduce Lyssa to the children, and that they would like to engage in a discussion with the children about what it

means to be in a wheelchair and answer any questions they might have. They feel that this will help the children and Lyssa get off to a good start. You agree, and the introduction and discussion go well. In fact, the children are fascinated with the wheelchair and love to take turns pushing Lyssa around in her manual wheelchair in the classroom and racing her while she uses her electric wheelchair on the playground. Their interest is so strong that they ask many questions about how wheelchairs work, where you can get a wheelchair, and numerous other questions. You decide to develop a thematic curriculum unit around transportation and specifically, wheelchairs. What resources are available to you? How will you align your unit to the learning standards in your state? What is your overall learning goal for the children? What are your learning objectives for each lesson? How will you assess whether the children have met the goals and objectives?

5. Jessie is a child in your preschool classroom. You have noticed that she is loud. She always seems to be yelling instead of talking in an "indoor" voice. In addition, she appears to be quite clumsy. The children are frequently complaining that Jessie is knocking down their carefully built constructions when she walks by, or knocking into their arms while they are painting at the easel. You are perplexed because you have asked Jessie to lower the volume of her voice numerous times. You have also asked her to watch where she is going when moving through the classroom. These requests do not seem to have made a difference and Jessie does not seem to be intentionally trying to irritate others. In fact, Jessie frequently seems to be confused when moving about the classroom, particularly during transition times. How can you assess what is happening with Jessie? Can you use FBA to help you? Are there other factors to consider when attempting to determine how to help Jessie?

4

Classroom Management with Special Techniques for Managing Challenging Behaviors[1]

Bridget Amory

In this chapter we will discuss how to set a positive environment for children's appropriate behavior. We will see the differences between disciplining a child and managing behavior. We'll look at examples of the ways the classroom organization, rules, and routines contribute to encouraging appropriate child behavior. We'll see examples and tools for preventing challenging behavior, as well as suggestions for dealing with disruptions, and ways to use functional behavior assessment (FBA) for special situations. Finally, we will encourage reflection on what to do to ensure smooth professional practice and growth.

Stanford entered kindergarten as a happy 5-year-old with a brand-new book bag on his back. He skipped along at the start of the school year meeting new faces and making new friends. He learned to sit crisscross applesauce on the classroom carpet during circle time. Through play, he learned to identify letters and numbers, and to exercise the patience required to learn how to wait his turn. Midway through the school year, however, things began to change for Stanford. He began to exhibit signs of frustration throughout the classroom. He became impatient when working with others and began to shove learning materials about whenever he

FIGURE 4.1 5-year-olds going to school.
Source: iStock

did not master a skill. When shoving materials didn't alleviate his frustrations or get the attention he was seeking, he began throwing them. The teachers first addressed the behavior by trying to ignore the misbehaviors and overall disruption to the learning environment. When the behaviors continued to escalate, the teachers began coaching him by labeling the behavior and providing him with a replacement activity such as kneading dough, coloring, or working with another toy. When the behavior progressed from shoving and throwing the learning materials to shoving classmates, the teachers knew they needed help.

Throughout this chapter, we will explore strategies and techniques teachers in the early childhood classroom can use to help children like Stanford who present with challenging behaviors.

Creating a Positive Learning Environment

What you can expect to find in a positive early childhood learning environment:

- Consistency
- Respect

- Harmonious atmosphere
- Sense of family
- Culture of learning
- Positive interactions
- Nurturing feedback

The effective teacher fosters a positive learning environment for all students. One way to support this is to ensure a high level of connectivity between the teacher and the child. Research begun by Robert C. Pianta at the Center for the Advanced Study of Teaching and Learning at the University of Virginia to create the CLASS (Pianta et al., 2008) established the idea that the relationships between teachers and children affect both child academic progress and social-emotional development. Teachers who know their students and treat them as individuals can affect their progress. While there are numerous ways for teachers to get to know their students, observation remains the preferred approach in the early childhood classroom. Allowing for children to explore and navigate their learning environment at their own pace will help you begin to understand how they interact with and respond to their world. An additional strategy would be to engage the child in conversation as they explore. A recent study of preschool teachers (Williford et al., 2016) showed that teachers who spent individual time with a child displaying externalizing challenging behavior may affect the ways in which teachers perceive children as individuals. Opening dialogue with a child often allows the teacher to enter the child's world at their level. One might approach a child by merely asking, "What do you find interesting in the classroom today?" While that question could be a bit high-handed for some young children, if the first attempt doesn't work, keep modifying your opening gambit just a little each time until you can engage the child in conversation. "What are you doing? Wha'ya working on? You building something today? Painting? Creating something? What are you thinking about? How'd you think of that?" Engaging children in conversations tends to help children feel a genuine level of interest on behalf of the teacher, which leads to developing a sense of trust and respect as the relationship continues to grow.

Creating an emotional climate that is appropriate for all students and their needs is essential to the functionality of the classroom. Getting to know students as individuals, being sensitive to their unique needs, allows teachers to foster strong relationships between themselves and the learners. The teacher needs to work to balance the role as the authority figure in the classroom while sharing their joy of teaching and learning with the students. This is a delicate balance. Practice has proven that when students know they are genuinely cared about and can relate to their teachers, their relationships deepen. When trust and respect are established through deep relationships, students are more willing to take learning risks. These learning risks will be taken only when the environment is positive, appropriate for the learning tasks requested, and conducive to student learning. Learning risks include behaviors such as Donald trying a math problem that he finds difficult or Mike speaking before the whole class, even though he is shy and this is difficult for him. Students often explore the limits of their behaviors in a safe environment. Think about it: What kinds of things are you willing to do for the people you like and trust, as opposed to the people whom you either distrust or don't feel like you know well enough to have formed an opinion about? It is human nature to do more for those you like and trust. We adults instinctively know this; so do children. Don't underestimate them. According to Williford et al. (2016), preschool teachers who spent individual time with children displaying externalizing challenging behavior were able to decrease their negative interactions with the children so that they had fewer clashes with teachers around their behavior.

Being a reflective practitioner is one way to assist in helping to create a positive learning environment. It doesn't mean just thinking about the high-level pedagogy business; it's also about all the little things that go into making up each school day. Reflection questions to consider when working to create such an environment include:

- Did I spend time speaking individually with each child today?
- How do I show them I am listening to them?
- Do I model the conversational model that I want the children to learn and use themselves?
- Did I smile today?
- How did I greet them at the beginning of the day? Say goodbye at the end?
- Do I know which of my students like and/or need a hug every day and which do not?
- Have I established a positive relationship with each student in my class?

- Is my attitude about learning and this class positive?
- Do I provide opportunities for students to know and accept each other?
- Do I have clearly defined and communicated classroom rules and procedures that were developed with student input?
- Do I have students identify their own standards for comfort?
- Do I help students develop positive attitudes about classroom tasks?
- Do I help students understand why knowledge is important?
- Do I help students recognize that they have the ability to complete the work?

Ensuring there is a clear sense of order, functional rules, and consistent discipline throughout the classroom also supports a positive learning environment. When you monitor student behavior and deal with any misbehavior in a timely and constructive manner, your students will be positively reinforced. Frequent positive reinforcement of appropriate and model behavior assists all students in remaining engaged with one another and their learning tasks.

FIGURE 4.2 Teacher thinking.
Source: iStock

Another way to create a positive learning environment includes regularly supporting cooperative learning opportunities for students so they feel cohesive and see themselves working together. Ensuring the classroom is relatively free of any friction and animosity will assist in promoting a positive learning environment. Where there is a clear sense of equity and fairness, relationships among students will be supported.

Establishing and maintaining high expectations and holding students accountable for their learning and behaviors are often among the first steps in establishing a positive learning environment. There is a desirable balance between socialization, play, and learning throughout the early childhood classroom. While the teacher often emphasizes the learning and task orientation consistently, there is a desirable balance that is created. This balance must include enough opportunities for socialization to support and foster relationships throughout the classroom.

Managing the Early Childhood Classroom

As teachers, while thinking about curriculum, instruction, standards, and differentiated instruction, we must keep in mind the most fundamental responsibility of classroom management: the maintenance of order to support safe and productive learning environments. A summary of the foundational knowledge, skills, and dispositions for accomplishing the maintenance of order is summarized in the following.

Foundational Principles of Classroom Management for All Children

- Be available emotionally and socially for children.
- Know the children and families you teach.
- Appreciate the strengths of each child.
- Establish personal relationships with children.
- Model respectful interactions with the children.
- Develop the rules with the children.
- Follow up rule infractions with consequences appropriate to the individual.
- Use specific language when applying positive reinforcement for desired behavior.
- Seek and use consultation for children with externalized challenging behavior.

Effective teaching and learning cannot happen without effective management. Did you know that effective teachers focus on management while ineffective teachers focus on discipline? Classroom management and discipline tend to be perceived as going hand in hand, although with effective management, one will not need to focus on discipline. Classroom management comes with the establishment of procedures and routines to provide structure throughout the learning environment. Discipline is the practice of training children to obey rules or a code of conduct. These structures are critical to the learning environment and assist in not only academic but also social skills.

Ultimately, it is the teacher, in collaboration with the students, who establish the classroom procedures and routines. Together, they are ultimately responsible for making the management of the classroom a productive and effective learning environment.

The tone of voice you use every day will help shape the learning climate in your classroom. For example, it is never okay to use sarcasm with young children—even when you believe a child may appear smarter or more mature than you expect. Some students might understand it and some may not. Most do not. But, one thing they do all get is the tone of your voice. Even infants recognize the tone of a voice. Think about how many different ways you can say "What are you doing?" or "How'd you think of that?" As you alter the emphasis to a different word each time you say those things, the meaning changes dramatically. In your classroom it will become more about how you say it than what you say. For example, Ms. Kathy was shocked when she heard Coco telling her mother that "Ms. Kathy yelled at us today." Ms. Kathy had no recollection of yelling at the children that day, and in fact prided herself in never yelling at the children in her care. Later, she realized that the children interpreted her stern tone as "yelling," even though she did not raise her voice. The sternness the children heard was interpreted as a yell. Author Maya Angelou has said "People will forget what you said, People will forget what you did, but People will never forget how you made them feel." This holds all the more true when communicating with children.

Strategies for Organizing the Physical Environment

Children thrive in routine and predictable environments. One way to support this is by ensuring a classroom that is thoughtfully structured and organized. You will want to do everything you can to minimize areas in

FIGURE 4.3 Early childhood classroom.
Source: iStock

the classroom that are difficult for you to monitor. The physical organization in the classroom includes the use of tables and shelves in a creative manner. Rearranging the environment can often fix a problem for an individual child or for the class. Sometimes it is a simple fix such as turning a bookshelf around or adjusting tables to sit at different angles. When planning for the physical layout of your large furniture pieces, it may be helpful to stand in the classroom in various locations to ensure you can see how traffic flows from each section of the classroom and to anticipate any potential problems. The physical organization of the classroom can help support students by providing easy lanes of movement throughout the classroom. Imagine yourself as one of your students and think about how they may find avenues to move throughout the classroom. Sometimes the tiniest space is where they find themselves trying to navigate and compete among peers in search of a coveted classroom resource or material.

Retired kindergarten teacher Mrs. Carlson reminisced about her mistake when first trying to organize her classroom. She explained:

> I had finally collected a rolling-cart closet to help with storing classroom materials. It was continually moved throughout the classroom and often ended up in the back of the classroom. One

day kindergarten student Ben reported "Lindsay is behind the closet, showing Jason her ba-gina."

Smiling, she continued:

> You see, Ben's dad was a local obstetrician so Ben knew what he was talking about. It happened about thirty years ago, but it left an impression. On me, at least. I don't know how Jason held up over the years!

Mrs. Carlson is able to laugh at her memory now, but at the time, she cringed when she realized that with her rolling cart, she created a hiding space for children that she could not monitor. Bottom line: It is critical to support ease of movement throughout the classroom to ensure the ongoing monitoring of students and to be ready to provide students with feedback as necessary.

The use of instructional charts throughout the classroom may serve as decoration as well as instructional tools. The physical resources displayed throughout the classroom can be used to support students during transitions to reduce any idle time. For example, various posters may be on display throughout the classroom and children may be asked to locate specific shapes or colors included in them. The inclusion of posters or photos that exhibit specific facial expressions associated with emotional responses may also help students to learn to identify and express their feelings. Learning materials should be organized and displayed in an accessible manner for children. The use of color coding, baskets, trays, buckets, or boxes may assist with this. A shatterproof classroom mirror hung at students' height is a wonderful tool to support this as well. Additionally, young children love to see their work on display. Working to regularly display student work will help fuel positive energy and the celebration of learning progress throughout the learning environment.

The effective teacher organizes a physical learning environment for all students. It is important to recognize that not everyone will find this easy to accomplish. For a teacher who is struggling, a good way to seek help is to get advice from an administrator or mentor teacher. This help could be sought by asking, "I want to arrange my classroom furniture and activity spaces to maximize learning potential. Is there someone on staff who is really good at that who might be willing to help me?" You are encouraged to ask for help with specific needs from your colleagues. Also know you will need to teach the children you have, in the classroom you've been assigned, with the stuff you've been provided. While you may be able to cozy up to a custodian and ask him or her to be on the lookout for decent furniture castoffs, sometimes (particularly when you're new) you just have to learn to make do. Don't let it get you down: Find stuff. Make stuff. Make do. Becoming resourceful as a teacher could become one of your greatest strengths. Ms. Sasha recounts the first day she walked into her classroom and discovered she did not have a classroom library, classroom materials such as markers and crayons. or premade posters for her wall. She quickly went to the public library and checked out books for her classroom library. She also stopped at her local reuse and recycle center for teachers and gathered bags of free materials for art and writing. Finally, she asked the children to create "all about me" posters for their classroom walls. Those posters became the first wall decorations in the classroom—as well as a meaningful message that the children were important and an integral part of the classroom community.

Being a reflective practitioner is one way to assist in helping to create such an environment. Reflection questions to consider when working to create such an environment include:

- Do I have the necessary furniture and materials to support my vision for an optimal learning environment? How do I acquire them?
- Do I know the expectations for managing paperwork and attendance for my classroom well enough to include the students in the process?
- What are the procedures for early dismissals and/or late arrivals?
- What are my classroom and building procedures for accessing the school nurse and/or the school counselor?
- Do I have all of the necessary learning materials readily available and easily accessible for me and my students?
- Do I have resources and activities to draw upon if I complete my lesson early or need to help refocus the students?

Establishing Procedures and Routines

Communication and consistency is critical when establishing procedures and routines in an early childhood classroom. While there are many 5-year-olds who like to hold up their hand and tell you their age, there are also those 5-year-olds that hold up their hand and tell you they

FIGURE 4.4 Children walking in a line.

Source: iStock

are a whole handful. This example is a subtle reminder from our youngest learners that when developing classroom rules, it is recommended to not exceed more than five at a time. This helps to ensure that you and the students can easily recall them without becoming overwhelmed. Having just a few clear, simple, non-negotiable rules that children understand is the goal. If you feel you need more than five rules, do not post more than five at a time. The rules need not cover all aspects of behavior in the classroom, just the priority areas. When developing them, remind yourself and your students you have the right to replace a rule with another as needed. As a new rule becomes necessary, replace an older one with it. The rule you replace is not suspended; it is retained as an "unwritten" rule which the students have learned and internalized. The students are still responsible for the rule you have replaced. Sample rules and meaningful consequences may include:

- Students will walk while in the classroom or hallways.
  - Students will go back and practice by retracing their steps by walking.
- Students will not talk when the teacher or others are talking.
  - Students will describe the appropriate behavior.
- Students will raise their hands for their turn.
  - Teacher will not respond to children who have not raised their hand.

One of the best rules—which works for young children, and adults—is a clearly stated "No mean stuff." Bottom line, if all of the strategies you have tried are not necessarily working, you need to go with what does. "No mean stuff" is something that is clear, to the point, and a powerful reminder that we all need to make an effort to get along. Also of note is the distinction between procedures and rules. Sometimes teachers will include in their "rules" things that are better thought of as *procedures*, such as, "This is the way we line up when it's time to leave the room." Compare that to the broadly applicable *rule*, "No mean stuff."

Prevention and Strategies to Stay Ahead of Behaviors

Managing groups of young children is challenging in itself. When a student presents with a challenging behavior, it can challenge a teacher both professionally and personally. It is imperative for teachers to remember that when a student acts out, it is not necessarily a personal attack. Students develop unique relationships with their teachers. These relationships allow for students to find strengths and weaknesses in their teachers. Many students use this knowledge to foster the relationship and strengthen it. Others may use it against teachers, and yet others may use this knowledge to ask for help. This may come in the form of consciously asking for help or acting out with behaviors as a method of asking for help.

Remember Stanford? As his teachers began to investigate his dramatic change in behavior and increase their communication with his family, they learned that Stanford's biological mother had been arrested and jailed during the winter holiday break. Stanford was told his mother "had gone off to college" without saying good-bye. This situation made him mad, sad, confused, and scared. The only way he knew how to communicate those feelings was by acting out among those he felt cared for and loved him.

Consistency

While there is a belief that if you focus on management you will not necessarily need to focus on discipline, it does not always work that way. The case in point would be Stanford. His classroom teachers had excellent management skills and yet he continued to act out and needed "discipline" because of factors far beyond his control. Consistency in teacher behavior may assist with this. When a student's mother suddenly "goes off to college" over the holiday break, all the initial plans for classroom management must be reconsidered.

Consistency in the classroom is not "everyone always gets the same thing." Nor is it "to each according to their needs"—at least not all the time, because there are times when, let's face it, that's just not fair. A balance of consistency and fairness is a tough row to hoe, but it's a goal we should all strive for. Consistency means that the children know what to expect from you, that you do not run hot and cold. You must present yourself as levelheaded and welcome your students with a smile and a positive, empathetic attitude no matter how tough your own world may be.

Supporting Individuals

Some examples of the ways you can assist individuals who need behavioral support that fit within the realm of still being consistent are described by Causton and Tracy-Bronson (2015). For Juan, who talks too much in large groups, give him more chances to talk by asking him to tell five things about his weekend. For Harriet, who roams the room looking for the construction paper, ask her to pass out the flyers from the principal's office. For Katie, who always wants to direct the discussion of the story, give her other opportunities to lead. For Danny, who appears shy when asked to speak in circle, let him work with a partner to share; they can agree on what should be said and one can speak. For Merrill, who always dithers over starting to work, give him more options for tasks. For Merriam, who doesn't like her seat by the door, give her another choice to work in the back of the room.

Dealing with Disruption

Working with young children is bound to result in the occasional disruption. However, when disruptions begin to rise to a level of interference with the learning of others or jeopardize their safety, it is critical you know how to deal with them. Most importantly, do not panic when there is disruption. Remain calm and reassure the children they are in a safe environment. If the disruption is extreme, you may need to exit the area for their safety and seek additional assistance. Teachers should avoid reinforcing the disruptive behavior by drawing additional attention to it. Look within and consider every aspect of your reaction. Sometimes even a smile or laugh at a child's behavior serves to inadvertently reinforce it. Being aware of your response to the behavior is critical.

Choosing to ignore a behavior is a common classroom response. It is important in this case to recognize that the teacher should ignore the behavior but not the child. So, ignoring pencil tapping momentarily, but moving close to Chuck, accomplishes the avoidance of a verbal reprimand, but pays attention to Chuck's nervous energy. He stops tapping and refocuses attention to the lesson at hand. Ignoring the child will almost surely lead to escalation. Chuck might graduate to drum beating. Another strategy to address disruption is to begin teaching a replacement behavior to replace the problem behavior. Giving Chuck a piece of clay to shape as he listens to class discussion provides an outlet for nervous energy and allows him to receive the social acceptance he seeks. It is necessary to break the desired behavior down into finite steps in order to teach it. All relevant parts of the behavior must be identified and communicated to the child who is supposed to learn it.

Prior to modeling the behavior for students, the teacher needs to walk through the behavior, paying attention to each of the following steps:

1. Model the steps you have identified exactly as you would expect the students to do them.
2. Practice the expected behavior, including opportunities to practice the behaviors with routines. Frequent practice will help the child toward mastery.
3. Reinforce compliance with the expected behavior by using positive reinforcement (such as praise or a small token) when the student demonstrates consistent mastery.
4. Retrain the expected behavior if necessary. This is not to be done as a punishment, and is to be used as often as needed.

So, positive reinforcement is one of the tools you have to manage disruptive behavior. This tool works well when you have observed carefully and chosen a reinforcement that is meaningful for the child. Besides disruptions, another common issue in classrooms is the potential to create a power struggle between you and a child who is not complying with rules or routines.

Power Struggles

Classrooms are set up with the idea that the teachers have the power. They have expert power, and in early childhood settings they are taller than most children and physically imposing. If you wish to share power with children and thereby help them learn to function effectively in the social world of school and beyond, then you must understand how to help children learn to assert themselves effectively and when to do so. The foundation for this mentoring comes from the rules and structure that you have set for the class. Nevertheless, there will be times when young children will test the limits of the rules and routines. It will help you be more effective in managing these occasions if you recognize that the child is asserting thoughts and feelings from a personal perspective—and we already know that children's views are cognitively and socially different than adults. Thus, as we develop rules and routines, we must be mindful that the child's perspective may lead to an interpretation of these expectations

FIGURE 4.5 Teacher and child talking over a problem.
Source: iStock

differently, which may lead to power struggles unless we intervene quickly while respecting the child's point of view. As a reminder, be sure that your schedule and environment are appropriate for the learners, that you have set clear rules and routines, and that you regularly reevaluate and consult the children throughout the year to adjust and accommodate to situations and their growing maturity in self-management.

Then comes the day when Brad says, "No, I won't sit in the circle!" What do you do then? Your actions will set the tone for the class in the moment and going forward. Act, don't react. That is, "Well, Brad, we're going to read *Where the Wild Things Are*. Hope you will join us soon. It's an exciting story!" Later on, you will meet with Brad to try to understand his perspective for his defiant behavior. Perhaps he didn't want to sit by "a girl." Perhaps he was tired because his family went to a Blackhawks game the night before. Perhaps he was engaged in a puzzle and wanted to finish it. Or maybe he doesn't really know why he refused to sit. In that conversation, you acknowledge his point of view, but remind him that the class has a schedule and routine to follow—and that in social situations, people need to give and take.

Managing Power Struggles: Some Tips

- Move close to a child who has a history of defying the rules. Your presence can be reassuring.
- Let some things slide, and address them later. You don't have to notice every time the pencil drops.
- Relax and be calm in the moment, so that your anxiety doesn't promote escalation.
- Don't rise to the occasion. For example, "You're a witch," doesn't require a response.
- Don't try to reason "in the moment" of conflict.
- Divert attention from the defiant child and promote the ongoing activity.
- Allow the child to save face.
- Give children space to regroup and establish self-control.
- Provide a choice: "You can sit here or there."
- Use positive words when you address the disrupter: "I can see that you are angry."
- Label the emotion: "You seem frustrated."
- Provide a cool-down space in a corner of the classroom that a child can choose or that you can suggest.
- Conduct remediation conversation in private: i.e., don't humiliate the child in front of the class.
- Reinforce progress by praising self-control.

The bottom line is to remember that you are the adult who is managing the classroom and you do so effectively by being responsive to children who are learning self-control and ways to negotiate the social world. As part of this mentoring, teach children to disagree respectfully, and model ways to solve conflict with adults as well as peers.

Tips and Tools for Turning Your Day Around

- Charts and check-ins
- Clip charts
- Behavior charts
- Earns
- Silent signals

Ask Yourself, What Are My Classroom Procedures For?

- Putting away supplies and materials
- Dismissing the children
- Cues or signals for getting student attention
- Communicating with families
- Water breaks
- Bathroom breaks
- Pencil sharpening
- Lining up
- Playground
- Safety drills
- Lunch/snack procedures
- Movement/transitions throughout the classroom/school environment
- How I handle interruptions

After you have thought of many of these situations and tweaked the problem areas and issues, you will still need to adjust for children who require more support to comply with the classroom rules, routines, and classroom management structure.

Special Interventions

Some children don't respond to certain classroom management techniques, which makes it difficult for teachers to handle their challenging behavior. What can be done in such a context?

To help children with challenging behavior, whether the behavior is momentary or frequent, requires careful observation and intervention. When the behavior is chronic, it is more serious, since the child has discovered a way for the challenging acts to work. To understand why the behavior is working requires systematic data collection. The observation and analytical framework most often used is FBA. Behavior (what the child is doing) can be analyzed using the ABC principles. Antecedent (A), which is what happened before the Behavior (B), and the Consequence (C), which is what happens after the behavior. Let's take a common example that occurs daily in the supermarket: Mom is gathering groceries for dinner at 5 or 6 o'clock in the evening. She just picked Jonathan up from the child care center. He is tired and a bit cranky. The two scurry through the store and reach the long checkout line. Jonathan sees the candy and razor blades in the checkout aisle; he grabs the candy and Mom says, "Put it back; we're going to have dinner soon." Jonathan clutches the candy to his chest and screams: "I want it now!" He starts to run backward with his prize. The rest of the line of people begin to look with horror at Mom, who cannot stop her 4-year-old from grabbing candy. She gives in and tells Jonathan: "Just this once, you can have the candy bar before dinner."

So, we have the Antecedent (**A**), Jonathan grabbing the candy and Mom saying no. Then we have the Behavior (**B**), Jonathan screaming in the grocery store aisle, and (**C**) is the Consequence—Mom gives him the candy. What does Jonathan learn from this experience? Screaming gets me what I want. To change the behavior, Mom must change A (standing by the candy herself, so Jonathan can't reach it) or C, putting the candy back in the rack (ignoring the censuring onlookers).

In classroom situations, it is not always as straightforward to identify the Antecedent: What exactly triggered the outburst? What can be changed to minimize the Behavior? What will be more rewarding for the child's Consequence? When observing in classroom settings to see how to alleviate challenging behaviors, you must carefully identify their function. In the grocery store example, Jonathan could be screaming because he wants Mom's attention (imagine she is scrolling through text messages); because he hated the spinach and meatloaf

Functional Behavior Assessment

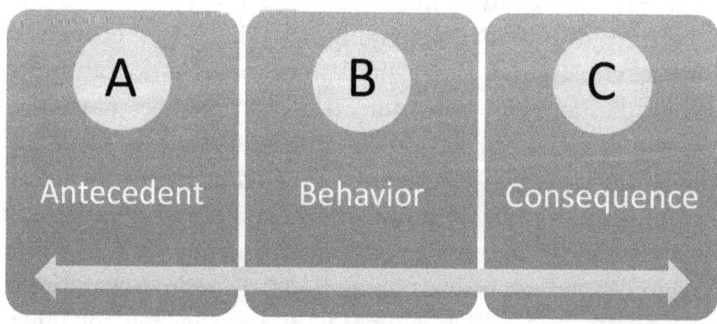

FIGURE 4.6 Functional Behavior Assessment starts with the behavior and works back to finding the antecedent, then adjusting the consequence.

Source: iStock

lunch and was asleep during snack, so he is hungry; because he is tired and wants the soothing taste of something sweet; or because he is bored and wants to be home. So the Behavior can function as a way to get Mom's attention, to relieve hunger, to get a treat when out-of-sorts, or to get Mom and others to hurry up and get him out of the grocery store. If we knew more about Mom and Jonathan and their history, or the particularities of the day, we could better understand the Behavior and develop appropriate Consequences.

So it goes in classrooms: Observation will lead us to understanding the function of the Behavior. Can we see or deduce the **A** accurately? Can we change the situation so that the Antecedent disappears? Can we change the **C**, so that we scaffold more successful Behavior? Often, challenging behavior occurs when young children have limited language, do not understand the environmental requirements, or rules and expectations are inconsistent. We can prevent some of the typical **A** factors by offering explicit instructions, prompts, and reminders, including visual schedules and behavior expectations; showing a child what will happen if the challenging behavior does not occur; decreasing environmental stimuli that a child finds noxious, such as loud noises or bright lights; offering choices; providing frequent access to preferred toys or activities (Meadan, Ayvazo, & Ostrosky, 2016, pp. 9–10). When children do not possess the language skills they need, you can help them replace challenging behavior by giving them non-verbal tools to request what they need or want. For example, using a language board to point to a desired activity or toy, teaching the child to gently tap an arm of a teacher or friend for access to a toy, or to teach a brief phrase, such as "my turn."

Once observation identifies the function of the Behavior, then we can modify the Consequence. So instead of giving a toy to the screaming child, you may need to remove the child from the activity while explaining the consequence and a more appropriate strategy. Table 4.1 shows an example chart from a preschool class, which summarizes an observation of Elijah's Behavior.

From the example, you can notice that the Consequence **(C)** the assistant teachers are applying is not calming Elijah down. As a side note: Elijah is 5 years old and very articulate for his age. The function of this Behavior is to gain the teachers' attention, and the emotional hypothesis is that Elijah is angry. So what would be a good technique to be used by the teachers to calm Elijah down?

TABLE 4.1

Time	A	B	C
8:00 a.m.	Elijah learns that Mr. Antonio, the lead teacher, cannot make it to class.	He argues with the assistant teachers and starts kicking and screaming.	Ms. Gaby, the assistant teacher, takes him out of the class and talks to him.
9:00 a.m.	Elijah is sitting in class playing by himself when the teacher tries to talk to him.	He argues and starts kicking and screaming.	Ms. Dianne, the other assistant teacher, takes him out of class and starts talking to him.
10:00 a.m.	The assistant teacher tries to have a conversation with him.	Elijah's behavior escalates and he starts punching the teachers.	Again he is taken outside to be talked to.

In such a situation differential attention (DA) would be the best solution to stop Elijah's tantrums. DA is a form of planned ignoring (Bayat, 2015). It might seem a bit absurd for a teacher to consider doing something such as ignoring a child. This is definitely not the intention of DA; rather it is ignoring the *Behavior* of the child as long as it does not cause any harm to the child or others.

Elijah was seeking attention and this attention came from arguing with teachers. In other words, being articulate for his age made him enjoy talking to teachers. The teachers' Consequences were reinforcing his behavior. How? When they took him outside of the classroom they were giving him what he wants, which is talking/arguing, and this is something Elijah enjoys. He was getting the attention that he needed and he was able to argue, which was something he also liked engaging in. It is worth noting here that children do not differentiate between positive attention or negative attention—most children with challenging behaviors just need attention. Now that we know what is reinforcing Elijah's behavior, it's time to change his behavior.

Scenario 1

To apply DA in such a setting, Elijah must *not* be taken out of class and talked to. As long as his behavior is not disruptive to the class, you can "ignore" his behavior. The trick here is that the moment he calms down, Elijah must get all the attention you can give from statements such as, "Thank you for calming down, I really appreciate it," to hugging him and giving him a sense of safety and security. Do teachers have to talk to the child? Yes, they do, but not on the spot. You give it time, a couple of hours and sometimes a day, then you remind him of what he has done and have a conversation with him about what went wrong and why he acted in such a way. Elijah will learn that the more he throws tantrums, the less attention he'll get; however, if he behaves well, then he'll get all the attention he needs.

Scenario 2

What if Elijah's behavior was disruptive to the class and hurtful to himself and others? If Elijah was kicking/punching/pushing another student as well as the teacher, you must give all of your attention to the child who got hurt and not to Elijah. The "victim" must be taken care of and made sure that they are alright. As for Elijah, DA is also applied but in a different way. Elijah must be taken outside of the classroom while you articulate that you will not talk to him until he calms down. You can sit next to him without giving him any attention, yet keeping an eye on him until his tantrum stops. Then, this is where praise kicks in: "Thank you for calming down, Elijah." He should be taken back to class and maybe after a while and after Elijah has calmed down (for example, in circle time), you can all discuss what happened and come up with a solution to whatever had caused Elijah to hit his friend.

What if Elijah was kicking and punching the teacher? Most teachers either ask the play therapist or a social worker to intervene or sometimes they call a child's parents to come and pick up the child—although you use exclusion as a last resort. Well, as a teacher, you can also do something about it. When a child such as Elijah is challenging you by punching or kicking, you must directly react by holding him from the back. In other words, you can wrap your arms around the child from behind so that the child won't feel he is being challenged. While doing this you then walk the child outside of the classroom, wait until he calms down, and then give praise. After things calm down, you can discuss what happened and make plans for an alternate solution in the future.

I like to think about DA as giving the child the attention that they need when the right moment comes instead of thinking about DA as a technique to "ignore" the child. It is all about the right timing. Usually child care centers and schools have consultants who can assist you with the observation and development of a plan for using FBA, for it is a technique that requires careful observation to understand the meaning of a behavior to the child. Elijah is a fairly straightforward example.

Elijah is one example of the children who present externalized challenging behavior. There will be other situations where determining the meaning of the behavior may take more observation and problem solving that may also involve conversation with the child, the family, and sometimes with special consultants. In addition to FBA, there are other special interventions you can use, such as a *special cue*, because Arthur has a developmental communication lag, or Rachel doesn't decode non-verbal cues, or Lesley's attention wanders easily.

Special Cues

To help children perform appropriately in the social situation of the classroom, you will need to provide prompts to assist individual performance. A variety of prompting techniques are available. These systematic strategies increase the child's probability of behavioral success. You can use direct or indirect verbal prompts. Direct prompts tell the child what

FIGURE 4.7 Teacher gesturing to a student.
Source: iStock

to say. So, for Mary Sue, you tell her, when she is reaching for Kathy's crayon: "Mary Sue, say 'May I borrow the green one, Kathy?'" Indirect prompts ask a question to provide a clue for appropriate behavior. So, for Gerald who is about to cut in line, you say: "Gerald, are you lining up in the right place?" Gestural or non-verbal prompts give the child a clue. Teachers have always used these kinds of clues, but they need to be understood by the particular child ahead of time. For example, Harry tends to always talk at a high volume, even when the class is working quietly at learning centers. He may try to get Marie's attention by asking loudly: "Can I use your ruler?" You cue him by making a walking motion with your fingers, so he knows that he should walk to Marie's desk to ask his question. Once he arrives at the desk, you show him the 3-inch sign, for soft voices used when talking quietly. Besides the quick verbal and non-verbal signs, you may need to use objects, pictures, drawings, or symbols as visual prompts. These prompts have to be personalized for the particular situation and child, considering age, developmental level, and the social setting of the class. Finally, modeling the appropriate behavior in full or in part can support the child's behavioral response. So, you show Marilyn how to sit in the circle, so she isn't sprawled in the middle or on top of other children. Physical prompts involve taking the child's hand or supporting a child's effort with an object. At clean-up time, you may have to lead Monroe to the table where he should sit, or show Mabel how much space she should leave between her friends in line (Meadan, Ostosky, Santos, & Snodgrass, 2013). The use of these prompts must be based on careful observation, yielding data to show where a particular child needs support, then developing a prompting strategy that is used consistently until it is no longer needed to support the child's behavior.

Positive Reinforcement

With all children, you can help them feel successful in their behavior by providing positive reinforcement, which is best delivered immediately upon your observation of the appropriate behavior. Types of reinforcement include verbal, gestural, social, and tangible. Take a look at these examples:

> **Verbal:** Rewarding a child with a positive statement such as, "What a great job you did in remembering to push in your chair!
> **Gestural:** Rewarding a child by giving a high five, smiling and nodding.

Social: Rewarding a child by tasking the child with watering the plants or allowing extra time with friends at a center.
Tangible: Rewarding a child with stickers or tokens.

For children whose behavior is challenging, you may need to increase the frequency for delivering this support. So, as you figure out why Jim makes noises when listening to the story, you give him a token for sitting quietly at intervals, perhaps starting with five minutes and gradually reducing the frequency as he is able to sustain attention without making noises. The tokens can be placed in your pocket or in a jar, so he can see that they are piling up, but the other children may not be fully aware of the purpose of the tokens. The tokens can be redeemed by Jim for a chance to take a book home, more time at the puzzle station, or a special treat provided by his family. These special supports need to be meaningful to Jim and his family.

Social Stories

A social story is a brief description of the protocol for appropriate behavior at a specific time and place. It is written for a particular child so that the child can be successful in a given setting. For example, Marvin doesn't know how to enter the play at the block center. He has frequently entered by knocking over the structures of his friends, so he can get their attention. As the teacher, you sit with Marvin and construct a story on "how to enter the block corner to play with friends." You describe the setting with who, what, and where, perhaps in the following way: "When we go to the block corner, we ask the children if we can join. We ask them what they are building. We ask if we can play, too. If they say yes, then I can begin adding blocks to the building. If my friends tell me that I cannot play with them, I can just build my own structure beside them." After the story is constructed, you can help Marvin understand the perspective of the other children. You can do this by including in the story, "When I knock the blocks down, my friends get mad." Conclude the story with ways to remember the story with something like this: "When we **ask** to join the play, our friends will usually include us." The social story sounds easy and straightforward, but it does take practice to write skillfully so that it provides a meaningful context for a particular child and gives the right amount of support. To read more about social stories and their use, see the work of the originator of the practice: Carol Gray (2010).

Video Recording and Discussion

One promising technique to help show children that they can perform a skill or function according to expectations involves video recording the child while they are behaving appropriately. Make sure to edit the video to show the child their best performance and discuss it with them. This technique is best used with children who are 4 years old or older (Buggey & Hoomes, 2011). This will of course work only with young children who are interested in viewing themselves on screen. In each of the special techniques described earlier you are individualizing your approach to children who present externalized challenging behavior. These are the children who need the most help from you as

FIGURE 4.8 Child watching a video with a teacher.

Source: iStock

a mentor, so they can become successful learners in the early childhood classroom *and* they may be the same children who may give you migraines or gray hair. However, your persistence in getting to know them as individuals and collaborating with specialists and families will pay off in the long run. You will be less frustrated when you use special techniques and most of all when you employ professional reflections.

Professional Reflections

A great way to monitor your progress as a teacher is to spend a few moments each day reflecting on the daily events. Regular reflection will assist you in problem solving, planning, monitoring, and adjusting as needed throughout your classroom. It will also assist you in making appropriate choices and recognizing problems to enhance the learning environment. Areas to consider reflecting on include the following:

- What worked well and why did it work well?
- What needs to be fine-tuned?
- What needs to be done to enhance this area?
- Are any additional human or material resources needed to assist in establishing the optimal learning environment?
- What did consistency look like today?

Additional areas to consider reflecting upon include discipline, management, lesson planning and delivery, rules and procedures, room arrangement, daily flow of schedule, time on task, student interest level, and student development of responsibility. A wonderful resource to capture these reflections may come in the form of maintaining a professional journal or blog so you can monitor your progress. Some successful teachers even keep these reflections along with their lesson plans as they work to refine and reflect for the future. It is important to note not every teacher is naturally adept at personal reflection. Some strategies to assist you with reflection include the following:

- You can simply talk to yourself while you sit in your classroom and look around.
- You can talk to yourself while you go for a long walk around the building (some people think better while moving).

- You can talk to an assigned mentor or other trusted colleague at your school. (Not all assigned mentors are the most trusted colleagues at any given time so be open to finding unofficial mentors among colleagues.)
- You can set up an outside "support group" that you regularly e-mail or phone. (Maybe you have a friend who works at a different school, a family member who's been in education, or a former professor you're close to.)
- You can start a journal or blog.

The message here is to remember you do not have to be alone in this process. Teaching and learning are highly social processes, after all. Making reflection a regular habit will help you grow as a professional. Do not wait until your principal or supervisor calls you in for a formal review to think about how effective you are, what's going well, and what you need to get better at—and do not view it as an "extra" thing that you may or may not have time for. Understand it as the powerful planning tool that it is. While you should not be afraid of abandoning processes and procedures that aren't working for you, you also need to keep in mind that you are dealing with small children who (typically) work best with structure and routine. So be cautious of making wholesale, willy-nilly changes in the way you run the classroom just to see what happens.

Finally, know that personal reflection is not a magical elixir. There will be some days when you are not quite sure why one thing went well and something else did not. You are working with people, after all, and people can be unpredictable. In addition, you cannot plan for every situation (unscheduled fire drill, a sick student, an unexpected visitor, etc.). No matter how proficient you are with your chosen reflection methods, building it into your daily routine will always be better for you than not doing it. There are only so many successes you can enjoy (and, by extension, your students can enjoy) if you continually fly by the seat of your pants.

Summary

Having clearly defined classroom procedures and routines is a common goal for what a teacher wants students to do. A routine, however, is what a student winds up doing automatically. Effective teachers teach procedures and students learn routines. Effective teachers dedicate a significant portion of time during the first weeks of the school year or class to introduce, teach, model, and practice procedures until they become routines. Developing the habit of reviewing daily schedules and procedures will assist you and your students with this. Communicating with students whenever there is a change in the daily routine will also assist with reinforcement. It is important to remember that changing behavior takes time. It is never recommended to yell or raise your voice with students to establish order. Instead, model and communicate your expectations consistently. Develop and teach signals to inform students when it is time to begin lessons or gain their attention. Do not expect students to learn all of the routines in one day. Procedures must be consistently modeled, monitored, taught, and retaught.

Take-Away Tips

- All children [require] responsive relationships, high quality environments
- [some] children will require targeted social-emotional supports
- [a few] children will require intensive intervention.

(Hemmeter, Fox & Snyder, 2013, p. 88)

Thus, to help children with challenging behavior whether the behavior is momentary or frequent requires careful observation and intervention. When the behavior is chronic, it is more serious, since the child has discovered a way for the challenging acts to work to personal advantage. Understanding why the challenging behavior is working requires systematic data collection.

Chapter 4 Activities

Jonas Smith

It is just after the winter holiday break and you learn you will be having a new student, Jonas, join your second-grade classroom. You do not have much information about him, but you know he has recently moved to the community with his mom, older brother, and older sister. You are told that Jonas's grandmother is an active community member. You excitedly prepare a new name tag, cubby, and folder for Jonas. Everything is waiting on his desk for him when he arrives for his first day. You tell your class you will be welcoming a new student and encourage them to be a good friend.

On the morning of his arrival, Jonas appears at your classroom door with the principal, Dr. Fry. Jonas keeps his head down while he shuffles his shoes on the floor. You greet Jonas with a smile and offer him a firm handshake to which he does not respond. Dr. Fry encourages Jonas to enter and says he will do just fine in his new classroom. She pats him on the shoulder and reassures him that he will be surrounded with new friends in no time. With that, Dr. Fry leaves you and Jonas to become acquainted. You invite him into the classroom and he reluctantly follows. The other children begin to swarm around and excitedly chatter about his arrival. You walk Jonas to his cubby to help him hang up his backpack. Again, he does not respond. You physically assist him in hanging up the backpack and lead him from his cubby to his new desk.

The students observe this behavior and begin to carry on with their usual morning routine, yet keeping an eye on Jonas. Upon arrival to his desk, Jonas continues to keep his head down and does not speak. You encourage him to take a seat at his desk and point out his new name tag indicating this is his designated desk. You show him the morning activity and tell him you will be right back. He slumps into the chair as you walk across the classroom to assist some of the other students. As you turn around to walk back across the room, you notice Jonas is now sitting up straight at his desk but is ripping apart the new name tag you have prepared for him. How does this make you feel? How do you respond to Jonas? How do you respond to the other students who are observing such behavior? What might your next steps be?

Throughout the week, Jonas continues to present behavior challenges in the classroom and across the school environment. He is defiant with authority figures and the children report he says mean and threatening things to them. While you have been unsuccessful in observing any of these alleged behaviors with the other students, you grow increasingly concerned about him and his interaction with his peers. One day on the playground a student reports "Jonas said he is going to kill me and blow up the school." What is your next step with Jonas? How do you respond to the student who reported the incident to you? What are your next steps with addressing the behavior concerns with the other students in your classroom? Their families? Your colleagues?

You immediately report the situation to Dr. Fry, who comes to the playground to remove Jonas. He is brought into the school and is joined by the school counselor, Dr. McDevitt. During the conversation with Jonas, they confirm he did indeed tell the student he was going to harm the student, himself, and if he could, he would blow up the school. They learn Jonas has a plan to carry out such acts. In order to access immediate mental health services for Jonas, the school needs permission from the family. The school contacts the mother, who says she is unable to leave work to come to the school to assist her son but will ask for his grandmother to come. The grandmother is contacted and indicates she will be to the school in a few minutes. During the approximate 45-minute wait for his grandmother to arrive, Jonas sits in the counseling office and wears a smirk on his face. He remains seated but rolls his head around and wrings his fingers as he fidgets in the chair. He persistently elects to not make eye contact with either Dr. Fry or Dr. McDevitt; however, when they are not looking directly at Jonas they can feel his eyes upon them. When his grandmother arrives to the school, she is greeted at the door and briefed on the situation. When she enters the counseling office and asks Jonas to look at her, he looks up and stares at her with a glare. He no longer wears the smirk on his face. She asks him what is going on and his response is a snarl where he states, "I hate you." She tells him "That is not nice" and kneels down to the floor to be at eye level with him. Just as soon as she is at his level, he lunges at her and knocks her to the floor. The two of them begin rolling on the floor cursing at one another.

The playground incident and the follow up family interaction place this child in a referral for a special education situation. What will be your role in facilitating the academic transition for Jonas? How will you reassure your class? What efforts will the school need to make with the families of your second graders?

Suzy Trumble

Picture yourself as a kindergarten teacher in an early childhood center. You have delivered your students to the school cafeteria for lunch. On your way to the staff lounge, you reflect upon the morning. Overall, it has been a productive day in the classroom with everything running smoothly. The students' behaviors are manageable; your lessons have gone well; and you are prepared to refuel for a promising afternoon. As you are sitting down with your colleagues to eat lunch, you are notified by the school secretary that Mrs. Trumble has arrived to pick up Suzy. You wonder what the message is about as you had not received notification of any early dismissals for the day. Setting your lunch aside, you report to the main office to meet with Mrs. Trumble. Upon arrival to the main office, you overhear Mrs. Trumble asking the secretary to call out Suzy from the bathroom. Confused, you quickly approach Mrs. Trumble and ask if everything is okay. After a brief conversation, you learn that Suzy experienced a stomachache during lunch. Rather than telling a lunch monitor of her situation, she asked to use the restroom. Once she was in the bathroom, she used her smartwatch with pre-programmed contacts to call her mom and ask her to come pick her up from school. Is this appropriate behavior for Suzy? Should there be a consequence for her behavior? What should the consequence be for Suzy? Is this an issue for family education? Are there policies in place that prevent child use of a smartwatch from being an issue in your school or child care facility?

Phillip Turner

It is October and you have learned that a third-grader is being moved from Ms. George's class to yours. Phillip has a long history of presenting challenging behaviors. Ms. Simpson, the school behavioral consultant, will be available to help you with Phillip and the family contacts.

Phillip displays disruptive and unsafe behaviors on a daily basis, on average every hour of the school day. He displays verbal outbursts and threats in the classroom and often throws chairs or other large objects, hits children, attempts to body slam or shoulder check students and teachers, overturns tables, and leaves the class without permission. Phillip threatens to kill or stab others or eat them ("I will make a meal of you"). Phillip frequently tells adults he will "get revenge" on them when he receives a consequence for any of these disruptive behaviors. Challenging behaviors increase when Phillip receives a consequence such as writing an apology letter or when being asked to do schoolwork that he claims is "boring." The behaviors also increase when Phillip perceives ordinary interactions (someone looking at him, walking past a student) as a threat and claims that the other person tried to hurt him or gave him a mean look.

Mrs. Turner reports that Phillip's behavior is similar at home and that he frequently throws his schoolwork out the car window. Phillip has diagnoses of attention deficit hyperactivity disorder and posttraumatic stress disorder; he witnessed the murder of his older sister three years ago and frequently talks about her death. Phillip occasionally tries to injure himself by banging his head on the wall or floor when upset. Phillip has exhibited all of these behaviors since preschool. Phillip is on his third behavior intervention plan this school year and has had 2 days of suspension and 14 absences for the current school year.

He pretends to shoot other students with his hand in the shape of a gun every day. He also frequently makes noises during instruction, such as screaming or yelling, "I hate this teacher!" and banging furniture during lessons. (For example, shoving desks, attempting to turn over tables, and shoving chairs).

During independent work, Phillip claims that he cannot do the work at all, even when other students or Ms. George come to his desk to offer help. He will say, "I can't do this!" or "I'm not smart enough!" or "This is too much work!" before attempting the assignment. Phillip complains of being "sleepy" and missing his sister. Phillip frequently cries at school and tends to scream while doing so. When Phillip appears to be happy, such as returning from being pulled out of class or finishing an assignment, he makes statements such as "I'm having a good day" or asks his teacher if he is having a good day even after behavior infractions or an emotional meltdown. In these instances, it appears that Phillip does not recognize or remember previous events from the day. He has returned 16 of 31 homework assignments and completed six assignments in class out of hundreds so far this school year. Phillip's standardized assessment scores show that he performs in the sixth percentile.

So, if Phillip were to enter your classroom in September, how do you prepare for Phillip's arrival? How will you use FBA to support your work? What assistance do you need from Ms. Simpson? How will you prepare your class for Phillip's arrival? How might peers welcome and support Phillip? How will you ask the children in your class to ignore his reputation? What do you think about the consequences Ms. George has used to try to modify Phillip's behavior? What questions do you have about other special services that Phillip may need to help with the trauma of losing his sister?

Note

1. For this chapter, Rafik Antar wrote the section on FBA.

5

Collaborating for Success

Megan Schumaker-Murphy

Although most of us went into teaching so that we could spend our days with young children, we are often required to invest an equal amount of time and energy into working with the adults in those children's lives. Building these relationships may not come easy to early childhood teachers—after all, we weren't fully prepared in how to educate and care for adults! This chapter will outline how positive family teacher relationships benefit us, as teachers, by decreasing children's challenging behaviors in class. In addition, it will offer ways to increase student performance and ease relationships with families. This chapter is set in the context of modern US family life and offers strategies to create and maintain positive teacher/family relations.

Why Should I Concern Myself with Relationships with Young Children's Families?

As a teacher, you are primarily responsible for children's learning. Why take on the burden of collaborating with children's families? Is it really a burden? What more can we do other than twice yearly conferences and report card pick up?

Ecological Systems theory teaches us that anything that happens adjacent to a young child has the potential to greatly influence that

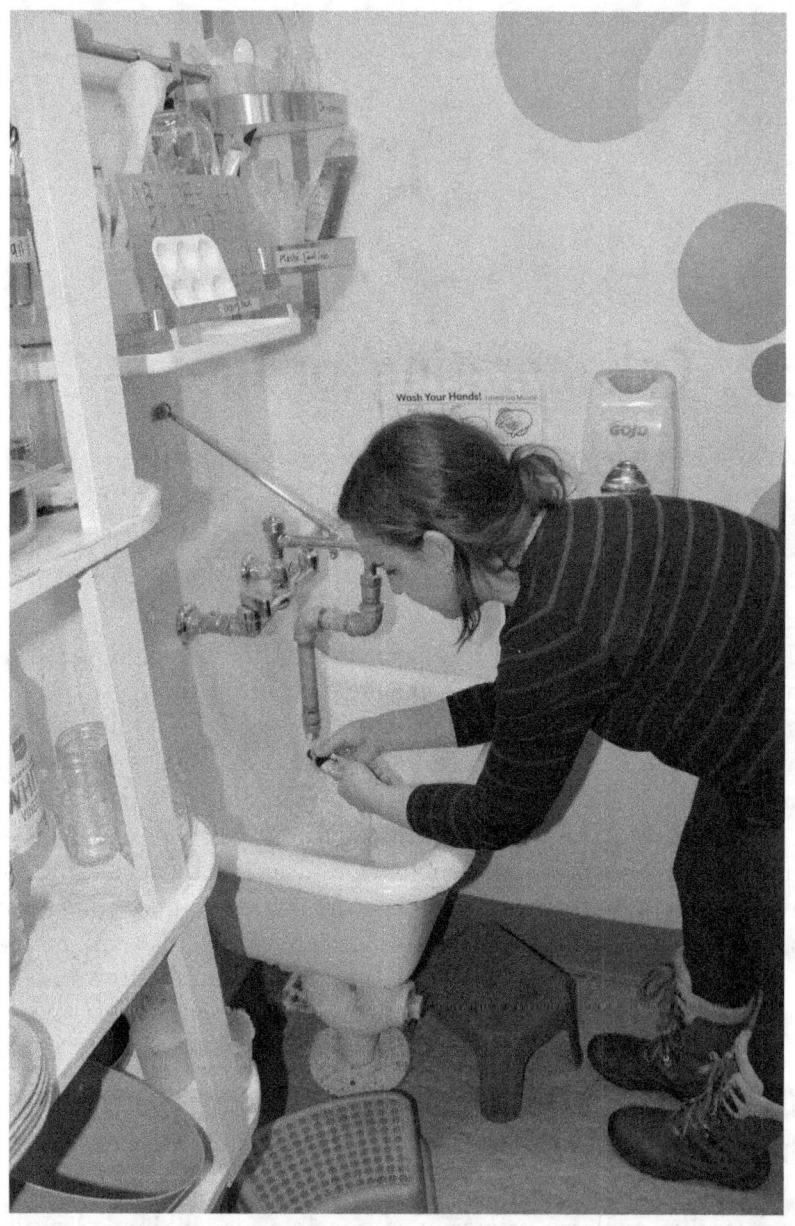

FIGURE 5.1 A parent washes paintbrushes so the teachers and teaching assistant can dedicate more time to interacting with the students in their classroom.

child's development (Bronfenbrenner, 1986). This means that we must work closely with families to support children. Not only does the educational environment impact the child, but also do the actions, beliefs, and values of their family and community. According to research, the most important predictor of how well a child responds to an educational or behavioral intervention is the level of family involvement and caregiver follow-through in that intervention (McWilliam, 2010). It is imperative for us to focus on building relationships with and support for families, especially in situations where behavior problems such as tantrums, hitting, and trouble engaging with peers are present. Involving the parents not only helps to build family capabilities (Ensher & Clark, 2011) but also pays off in the form of fewer classroom behavior problems.

Positive home/school connection is highly correlated with better student achievement (Galindo & Sheldon, 2012) and better social-emotional adjustment (Hughes & Kwok, 2007). It is not surprising that strong, healthy parent/teacher relationships are linked to a decrease in disruptive and problem classroom behaviors in young children (Serpell & Mashburn, 2012; Sheridan et al., 2012). When parents and teachers get along, children learn more and behave better, too. Another positive consequence of positive teacher/family relationships is these interactions help parents feel more confident in their abilities to help children with homework and other academic tasks (Green, Walker, Hoover-Dempsey, & Sandler, 2007). Supported families are also more likely to volunteer their time at schools—whether chaperoning field trips, doing chores, or helping with a special project. When we build parents' capacity to support children, we create a community of learners who learn meaningfully and achieve academically, and we recruit willing parents to help with classroom projects and tasks that take time away from our teaching. In fact, positive school/home relationships can change the attitudes families have about schooling; thus, changing the messages they transmit about the value of schooling and behavioral expectations to their children (Serpell & Mashburn, 2012).

Understanding Modern Families

Before diving into strategies for collaborating effectively with our children's families, we must first develop an understanding about what the modern American family looks like. In today's world, there is no such thing as a "typical family." Lacking a consistent template to guide our notion of what constitutes a family, it is best for us to not assume anything when it comes to family composition. A definition that I like to use is a family is a group of people (two or more) who have committed to being a family and work together to perform family functions including: making money to pay the bills, grocery shopping and meal prep, caring for children and pets, celebrating holidays, and providing emotional support for each other (adapted from Posten et al., 2003). Members of a family may be related through blood, marriage, or adoption but don't have to be. Members of one family may or may not live together. An example from my work in early intervention is when I worked with a family consisting of the biological parents of a toddler with special needs, Alexander. Alexander's parents were not romantically involved and each parent had older children. Alexander's father had a set of twins in high school and his mother had a daughter in elementary school. Both parents worked full time. Their family spanned two physical households that worked together seamlessly to achieve daily parenting tasks of all four children. The adults even shared the care of their older children, who had different biological parents. Alexander achieved all his special education goals and had the added benefit of generalizing skills across two familiar and safe home environments. Initially, I was confused when I didn't know which parent or teenager to expect on any given day, but family members themselves were never confused. Alexander was always dropped off on time in clean, weather-appropriate clothes and picked up on time, too. He was happy to see either of his parents or his teenage brothers at pick-up time. I finally began to appreciate that I didn't need to know in advance who was going to be there with the toddler, because I knew that someone he loved and trusted would be.

In my decade-long career, I have worked with many different kinds of families, including those who are experiencing divorce, single-parent families, military families, same-sex couple–headed families, families in which the grandparents or another blood relative are caring for the children, families in which several generations live in one house and share in all the care for the children, families with stay-at-home fathers, families with incarcerated parents or siblings, foster and adoptive families, families that consist of two female friends living together in order to share child care and pool financial resources to afford a home in a good neighborhood, families that are experiencing mental health and addiction challenges, families with undocumented immigration status—and perhaps, once or twice, the perceived ideal nuclear family with married, heterosexual parents, a stay-at-home mother, two children, and a dog. In your classroom, you may experience all these family situations or just a few. Regardless, as a teacher, you will need to examine your beliefs and expand your horizons in thinking about families in all their permutations.

For children's families to feel that your classroom is a safe and comfortable place within which a positive relationship will flourish, all types of families must feel that you understand and accept their individual family, however each family may be comprised. It is for this reason that in this chapter, I will refer not to parents but families. I suggest you make this change in your vernacular as well. Changing this one simple word in your written and verbal communication to families sends the message that your classroom is an inclusive space that welcomes all types of families and all adults who take on caregiving responsibility for the children in your classroom. It also invites all caregivers with a personal stake in your children's well-being into your classroom support system. When there is a behavioral concern such as tantrums, swearing, or hitting, there are more adults in the child's life who are implementing behavioral modification strategies. The more people who implement interventions, the faster the behavior will become extinct! The foundation of inclusiveness sets the stage for collaboration between families and teachers. Family/school collaborations may include parents volunteering to chaperone a field trip, a grandparent who takes part in a classroom celebration, or a school-wide team of people and family members implementing a behavior plan for a child or a reading intervention for a child.

Once you understand the composition of a family, you can begin to examine how families function. Family functions include all activities that families engage in on a daily or consistent basis to meet their collective and individual needs. Family functions include providing for the economic needs of the family, daily care activities (child rearing, cooking meals, doing the dishes, laundry), recreation (watching television, going to the movies, reading books together), education (choosing a school, getting the child there on time, making sure that homework is done, finding a tutor or seeking special services when a child is struggling), affection (physical affection like hugs but also loving words and encouragement), socialization (having play dates, making and maintaining friends, joining clubs, supervising social media), and identity development of self and family (family's values, religion, home language, goals and expectations for children and their behavior) (Turnbull, Turnbull, Erwin, Soodak, & Shogren, 2015). Each family meets these needs and prioritizes how to allocate family time to each task differently based upon their own family culture and values.

Remember Alexander? In his family, his parents each worked and met their own household's financial needs. Alexander's school fees were a shared expense paid for by two checks, one from his mother and one from his father. The family had a strong Afrocentric identity that was consistent across homes. Music was an important part of family life. The family celebrated holidays together and enjoyed frequent family dinners in the father's house because he had a bigger dining room table. It was common for Alexander's twin brothers (biologically related to Alexander's father only) to spend the weekend with Alexander's mother or for Alexander's father to pick up Alexander's sister (biologically related to Alexander's mother only) when he took Alexander for the weekend. Both of Alexander's parents attended Alexander's early intervention meetings and Alexander's early intervention therapists alternated sessions at school and each of Alexander's homes. Group text or e-mail was utilized so that each of Alexander's parents knew exactly what was happening during Alexander's therapies all the time. Alexander's mother told me that she and Alexander's father had merged the calendars on their phones to ensure that there were never miscommunications about where each parent needed to be. So, this family created a smooth and even way of handling the functions to make their family work for Alexander and themselves. For other families, the functions may be carried out differently.

Every family has their own unique family culture with its own strengths and challenges that determines how family functions are carried out and what priority each function has within the family system. For many families, economic needs are the focus of family life. This is especially true for families with children with special needs or those caring for ailing grandparents. Consider Andrea, who is 4 years old. Andrea's 3-year-old brother Jaime has multiple significant special needs. Jaime attends a half-day preschool program in their school district. Their mother, Liliana, can't find appropriate and affordable child care for Jaime so she is unable to work. The family relies on government assistance to make ends meet. Andrea's class has a field trip to the zoo coming up. Liliana is unsure she will be able to pay the $10 field trip fee and is trying to plan meals with ramen noodles and peanut butter for the week so the family can spare $10 for Andrea to go on the trip. This week, as Andrea's class is readying for the field trip, they are working together to create an animal alphabet book. Andrea is working on a page in the class's animal alphabet book when she suddenly gets up, crumples her paper, and throws it across the room. "This is stupid and I hate animals," she yells. Andrea is feeling the tension of the family's economic crisis. The way in which Liliana handles this crisis will show support for Andrea or exacerbate her stress. As Andrea's teacher, it will be helpful to know about the family's economic stress and the ways they are coping. Whether your school has funds to support children such as Andrea will also shape the collaborative relationship that you may form with the family. Some families may not want you to know of the economic stress, but Andrea's behavior related to it will influence classroom behavior. Thus, collaboration with families may reveal stresses or not depending on the way the family functions in meeting economic and other needs.

For Andrea's family, the way in which economic stress is handled and the collaboration that you are able to establish will influence the long-term outcome of Andrea's developmental and educational progress. Studies show that a high income level is a much more significant predictor of family quality of life than is the severity of a child's disability (Davis & Gavidia-Payne, 2009) and that for some families, adequate financial resources completely eradicate the potential stress caused by children's behavioral challenges. More money increases access to family supports including: therapy, high-quality child care, private schools, household help, and opportunities for families to participate in self-care activities likes trips to the spa, a personal therapist, or lunch with a friend.

Financial stress also often amplifies pre-existing difficulties in the family ecosystem, such as romantic-partner strife (Fiedler, Simpson, & Clark, 2007). Melanie and Raj have 3-year-old triplets and are committed to Melanie being a stay-at-home mom. Raj and Melanie have always disagreed about what faith to raise their children. Melanie was raised Lutheran and Raj is Hindu. After many months of arguments and the use of a family therapist to help the couple communicate, Raj finally agreed to enroll the children in the same Lutheran preschool that Melanie attended. When Raj's work hours are cut, he and Melanie fight over how to best cut their expenses. Raj wants to pull the children out the Lutheran preschool to save money on tuition but Melanie feels that the family can cut other expenses instead. Melanie is angry because she thinks that Raj is using their finances as an excuse not to send their children to a Lutheran school. Raj becomes defensive because he is trying to figure out a way the family can continue to have Melanie stay at home with the triplets now that their family income has decreased. The triplets overhear the arguments and cry hysterically every day when Melanie picks them up from school. How can you, as a teacher, support the triplets through this stressful time?

Thus, it is important for you to understand that you supporting only one of the basic family functions (education), while the family may have other functions that need the bulk of family resources such as taking care of a grandparent with Dementia or coping with one parent who has bipolar disorder. When families struggle to accomplish their family functions well, it is common for the resulting family stresses to trigger challenging behaviors in children at home and school. The most common of these behaviors are tantrums, sleep, and toileting disturbances, and becoming either aggressive or withdrawn with peers (Bayat, 2015). These challenges are often evident when families are experiencing food insecurity, homelessness, divorce, abuse, addiction, incarceration, and/or mental illness. For this reason, it is key for you to become familiar with the social services in your neighborhood so you are better able to help families find ways to function well. Local food pantries, free clinics, respite agencies, local faith communities, community mentors, free and inclusive local programming including library story time and parent groups, mental health services, and early intervention programs are examples of helpful resources.

While each family works together to accomplish the tasks associated with the family functions, the ways in which they accomplish these tasks are greatly influenced by culture. Although many of us view culture as simply what we look like, the language we speak, and the holidays we celebrate, it is significantly more complex. Culture is heavily influenced by geographic region, education, individual personality, religion, occupation, education, socioeconomic status, and ability or disability, as well as the time and sociopolitical context in which we live (Lynch, 2011). Our culture impacts our behavior, often without our implicit knowledge of its impact on our beliefs, values, and actions. Culture isn't static and varies within groups as much as between groups. Families may change faiths or become devout. The death of a family matriarch can bring about a change in Thanksgiving traditions. Being aware of the cultural backgrounds of the children you serve is critical for building collaborative relationships with families. Regular communication with families will serve children in your care to understand the ways that their cultural values are evolving.

Strategies for Building and Maintaining Successful Relationships

Become Culturally Competent

In addition to understanding the myriad ways that children's families may be comprised, you must also learn to work effectively with families from diverse cultural and linguistic backgrounds. In just over 20% of American families a language other than English is spoken in the home (US Census Bureau, 2010). In my daughter's Chicago public school, for example, there are 39 different languages spoken by the 1,000 students. Especially in urban school districts, many children who speak English natively are likely to have a cultural background different than their teachers. In Chicago, most of the public school teachers are White women while less than 10% of the students identify as White (Chicago Public Schools, 2016). To effectively collaborate with these families, we must keep in mind that cultural differences extend further than celebrating different holidays and eating different foods. Many families, even those that have assimilated into celebrating traditional US holidays like Halloween, call their parents something other than "Mom" and "Dad." I have worked with families that called their mothers Mommy, Uma, and Ema, and families that call their fathers Appa, Abba, Baba, Daddy, Tatty, Nana, and Nunu. Each of these families identified as American and celebrated US secular holidays or those that have become secular including Halloween, Thanksgiving, and Valentine's Day. Without asking, I would never have known the children used a word other than "Mom" or "Dad" to address a parent. When you take the time to ask what the children call their parents and work those words into your interactions with the families and children, this is an example of collaborating effectively to make everyone feel welcome. The National Center on Cultural Competence (2007) states being culturally competent requires that schools and teachers value difference and diversity, assess themselves to determine their levels of cultural competence, manage the dynamics of difference, learn about and integrate cultural knowledge into teaching and policies, and adapt to the cultural needs of the children and families being served. As teachers, our capacity to strive toward cultural competence will influence the relationships we build with families and ultimately the success of our empathetic relationships with children.

Our culture is so deeply engrained into each of us that it informs each one of the decisions that we make. Our culture deeply impacts our belief systems about school, teachers, the role of parents in a child's school, and appropriate early childhood behaviors. We can experience "culture shock" when we engage with others who challenge our own values, beliefs, and behaviors by displaying a very different (or seemingly different) set of values, beliefs, and behaviors (Lynch, 2011). Many of the challenges that teachers in diverse school communities face can be explained by cultural misunderstandings often resulting in culture shock. For example, many US teachers value parent involvement at the school level. Parent involvement carries such a value in the United States that it is a required component of the federally funded Head Start Preschool Program; however, many immigrants or first-generation families do not share this value and indeed view the school as solely responsible for the child's education. Some cultures, in fact, find it terribly disrespectful to insert themselves into school matters. Families from these cultures sometimes view teachers as experts and meeting with us is viewed to challenge our expertise. In other families, the mother is to stay at home and manage the household and children while the father is the "face" of the family. This does not mean that the mother does not value the school or support her children's education. In one suburban school, a mother who never once came to the school sent $100 to the school's Christmas fair despite the family not celebrating the holiday themselves. Sending the money was the way that this mother felt she could and should support the school. You may think that a family is not invested in their child's education because the family is not demonstrating their support for their children's education the same way that you would.

The most challenging step to becoming culturally competent in your teaching practices and interactions with families is to become self-aware of the ways in which your culture impacts your beliefs and actions. This is both an enlightening and frustrating activity. (See

Activity 2 at the end of the chapter for a sample activity to help grasp some of the infinite ways in which our culture shapes our every choice.) Once you fully understand how culture influences your beliefs and behaviors, you can begin to examine your own reactions to the actions of others rather than assigning those actions a value of good or bad.

After deepening awareness of your own culture, it is time to begin learning about the cultures of others. For this to be successful, you must cultivate an openness, appreciation, and respect for cultural differences (Green, 1982 in Lynch & Hansen). A preferred strategy is to view interactions with people different from you as learning experiences. During these interactions, observe the ways in which your communication partners (in this case, young children's family members) speak and use body language. Observe the ways in which caregivers interact with their children and each other. This provides insight into how families function. Ask families and children nonjudgmental questions about their daily life and family priorities. Questions should be utilized to gain an understanding of the families with whom you are interacting. Ask questions only with the express purpose of achieving this goal, not only because you are curious. This can be challenging. Once I began learning about other families and cultures, I wanted to know so many things about their family lives but I had to learn to balance my need to know about them with a respect for their privacy and dignity. I worked with several families whose marriages were arranged. I am very curious about arranged marriages and I would have loved to ask about all the details of these unions. These details weren't relevant to my work with their children, so I had to keep this curiosity to myself. Cultural information can be gleaned through books, art, and social media, although it is not advised to make assumptions about the ways in which an individual family will behave. There is a great deal of difference within cultures, often much more so than the difference between cultures (Lynch, 2011). Instead of making assumptions based on what you already know about families from similar backgrounds, allow families to teach you who they are. One strategy that is helpful at the beginning of the year is a short answer form that you can send home in registration packets with questions about children. Ask questions about what the child likes to be called at school and what the child calls her family members, who the important people are in the child's life, what the family likes to do for fun, and what events they celebrate. Forms like this communicate to parents that you are interested in learning about their child and family and sets the stage for open communication without prying into very private details about their home lives. If you are working with families who are especially private, you can make these forms optional.

Creating an understanding of the family and cultural compositions of each child's home life can seem overwhelming. Fortunately, early childhood classrooms are excellent places to explore what it means to be a family and learn how each child's family is comprised. One of my favorite units to complete in the beginning of the school year is the All About Me book. This creates an organic way for children to share cultural and family information with the class. A bulletin board with family photographs or student-drawn family portraits provides the opportunity for children's families to see how they are valued in your classroom community and to invite them to teach you and each other about themselves, while also providing evidence of the learning taking place in the classroom.

Even the most culturally competent teachers will sometimes make mistakes. Thankfully, many families will forgive your missteps if they know that you are trying. For many years, I worked in a Jewish Orthodox neighborhood in Chicago. The families I worked with varied

FIGURE 5.2 An example of a family photo wall.

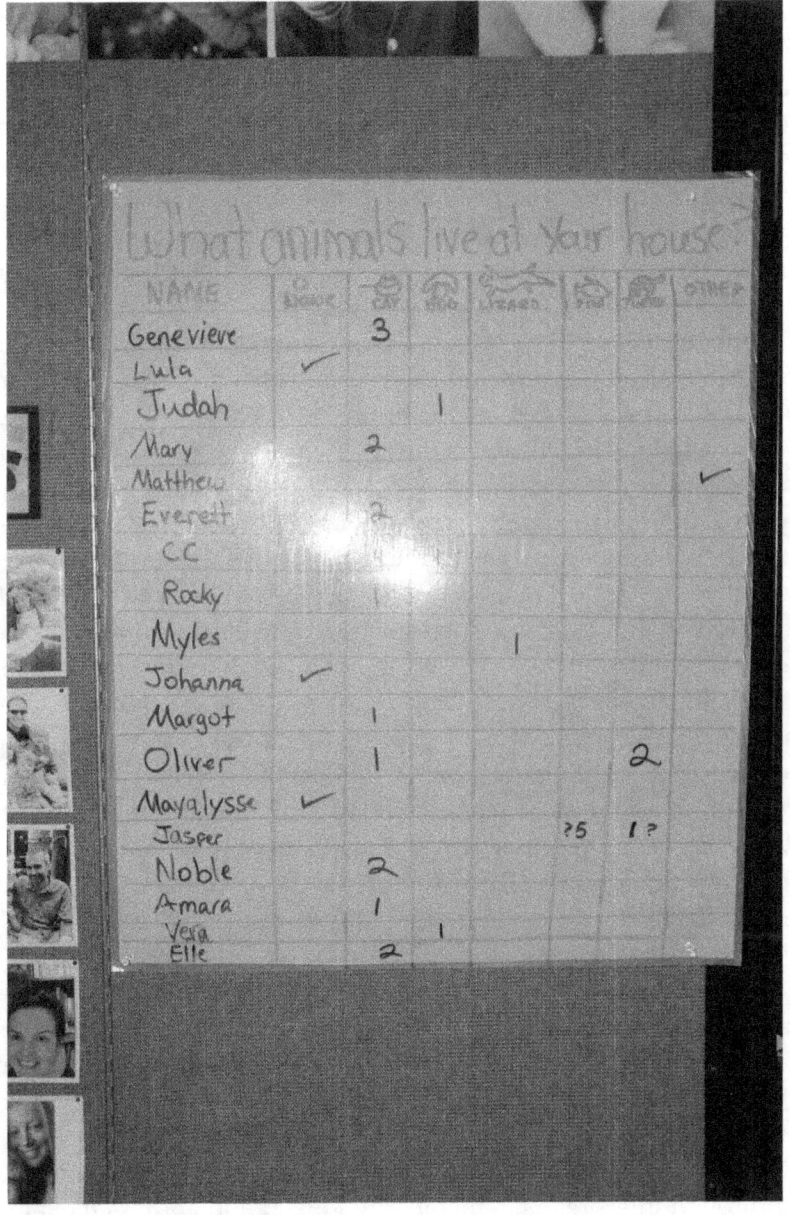

FIGURE 5.3 A preschool math activity can incorporate learning about children's family pets or home composition.

greatly in how they expressed being *frum* (the community's word for being devoutly religious and following the 613 Jewish laws) but each of them kept Kosher. Jewish holy texts and rabbinical scholars have outlined a set of strict rules about what animals can be eaten, how they can be prepared, and how a kitchen is kept. After five years, I thought I had a pretty good understanding of the culture and the rules of Kosher eating. I was assigned to work with a family that identified as *Moshiach*. The father was a *Moshiach* rabbi and the mother was the principal of a small *Moshiach* boarding school. Over the phone, the mother explained to me that no depictions of non-Kosher animals were allowed in the home. Kosher animals include only those that chew their cud and have split hooves (sheep, goats, bison, deer, elf, cows, and giraffes), non-scavenging birds (chicken, turkey, geese), and fish that have both fins and scales. I painstakingly went through my therapy books and toys to remove all materials with cats, dogs, bears, monkeys, etc. I went into the home and asked the mother to double-check my materials to make sure that I hadn't missed anything. She obliged and told me she was happy that I had made such an effort to make sure that I followed the family's religious views. I left the home feeling quite good about myself until I got into my car, looked down, and realized that my dress had non-Kosher seahorses all over it! I sent the family an apology message and the mother responded, "I knew you were trying so hard, I didn't have the heart to mention it! We really appreciate that you are trying." Because I had shown the family that I was committed to learning about and following their traditions, they were able to view this mistake as "not a big deal" instead of a disrespectful and potentially relationship-damaging action.

Often when working with diverse populations, you will experience language barriers. When this challenge occurs, ask a colleague if there is a known interpreter either on the school staff or at a community organization, or even an informal community leader. Communicating through a third party can be complicated but it does not have to interfere with family/professional relationships. When communicating through interpreters, remember to look at and address the family member you are speaking to, not the interpreter (Virginia Department of Behavioral Health & Development service, n.d.). Speak in short, clear sentences and use gestures if possible. Wait until the interpreter has finished translating what the family said to begin your response. If possible, provide any written information to the translator prior to

Collaborating for Success ◆ 143

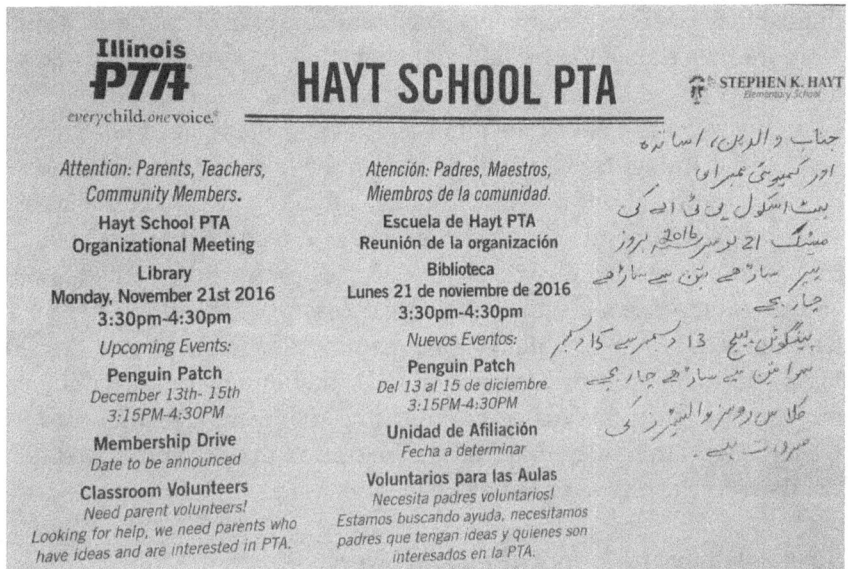

FIGURE 5.4 A Chicago school translates written communication into Spanish and Urdu.

the meeting so the translator may translate the English text into the family's native language. Whenever possible, send correspondence to families in their home language if they are not fluent in English.

Unfortunately, there will not always be an adult interpreter present. Unless it is an absolute emergency, the use of bilingual children to translate should be avoided. Discussions about young children's challenging behaviors should never be the responsibility of a sibling or even the young child. Instead, utilize distance translators, pocket translators, bilingual dictionaries, and online translating applications including Google Translate. Each of these resources is imperfect and will certainly not translate exactly, but attempting to communicate in the family's native language demonstrates your value and respect for them. For day-to-day communication about good news or the acquisition of a new skill, the use of work product, gestures, and facial expressions can be very helpful.

I successfully strengthened a relationship with a mother over silly translations from Google. Our regular translator was out of the country, so we attempted to rely on Google Translate to communicate back and forth in English and Assyrian. This was tricky not only because Google asked if I would enjoy a cup of the couch but also because Assyrian and

English have different alphabets. Each time one of us would type a sentence into the translator, we had to first change the language of the keyboard. It was painstakingly slow and cumbersome. The mother and I laughed over the silly translation and began using gestures to help convey our thoughts. This broke some of the tension that surrounded communicating about her son, Toma's, behavior, because the mother was worried about her son's progress and wanted to know how to help him by implementing my therapeutic suggestions. And I wanted her to appreciate the role she would play in successfully disrupting the challenging behavior. So, while English communication was a challenge in our partnership for addressing Toma's challenging behavior, it was our mutual effort toward communicating that built a relationship as we were working together. Without an effort to understand each other, the therapeutic plan would have been less than successful.

Build Relationships Before a Problem Occurs

As seen in the previous section, the best intervention is prevention. "Prevention" in this case means building meaningful relationships with families that appreciates the ways families function and the role that culture and language plays in carrying out the family's business. As discussed earlier in this chapter, children with strong positive connections between home and school behave better in class and achieve at higher academic levels. Thus, it does not make sense for you to wait until a child demonstrates challenging behaviors to develop a relationship with families. Primarily, you should be aware of how you communicate with families. Parents overwhelmingly prefer working with early childhood professionals who are sincere, caring, supportive, nonjudgmental, and responsive to family concerns (Bailey, Hebbeler, & Scarborough, 2003; Hurtubise & Carpenter, 2011). Do the families you serve see you as a person as well as a professional who can empathize with their situations?

Take a moment to picture your reaction if a trusted friend called you to tell you that your child was caught throwing eggs at a neighbor's house. The friend is calm, nonjudgmental, and reflective about why your child misbehaved and offers strategies to help the child better understand the expectations next time. Now take a minute to imagine your reaction hearing about the same behavior from an irate neighbor that you have met in passing a few times but never really gotten to know. The neighbor is clearly blaming the egging on your poor parenting and demands that you come right over and clean the eggs off her garage and your child be punished. Which scenario would you prefer? As you communicate with families, keep in mind how you would like to be communicated with.

Building positive parent/teacher relationships should begin on the first day of school, if not sooner. If and when challenging behaviors begin, it is significantly easier to communicate these challenges to families when there is an existing relationship that was built upon a foundation of trust, collaboration, and shared value for the child and their education. You can facilitate positive family/school relationships in a variety of ways including sharing good news, creating a warm and inviting classroom environment, clearly communicating classroom expectations, and displaying evidence of student work. Student work can be displayed on bulletin board exhibits, class albums of activities, videos of children at work, etc. You can also be sure that you are available at the classroom door when children arrive to greet the children and say hello to families.

One benefit of the necessity of ensuring the safe drop off and pick up of children each day is the opportunity for brief interactions between the family and teacher. This time of day is excellent for a quick comment about how Emilio helped a friend up at the park or how Tanisha is now writing her name on her own. These small comments help communicate to families that you value their children, know them and their academic needs well, and take pride in their successes. It also establishes a pattern of communication between you and the family that occurs at regular intervals rather than only when a problem arises.

As part of the effort to engage families in the classroom and connect with them during pick up and drop off, care should be taken when designing classroom spaces to ensure that the spaces invite family engagement (Gonzalez-Mena, 2014). For example, if coat cubbies are located inside the classroom, a small bench can be placed nearby for families to utilize while children are bundling up. The coat cubby area is also an excellent space for a bulletin board where photos or drawings of children and their families can be displayed alongside notices of events and school happenings. You can encourage children to take family members around the classroom to show off what projects are in the works or where they sit during circle time. Establishing a comfortable space for families during drop off and pick up invites them into your classroom community, whereas standing in a doorway and sending children out to parents communicates the message that families are not welcome in your classroom space.

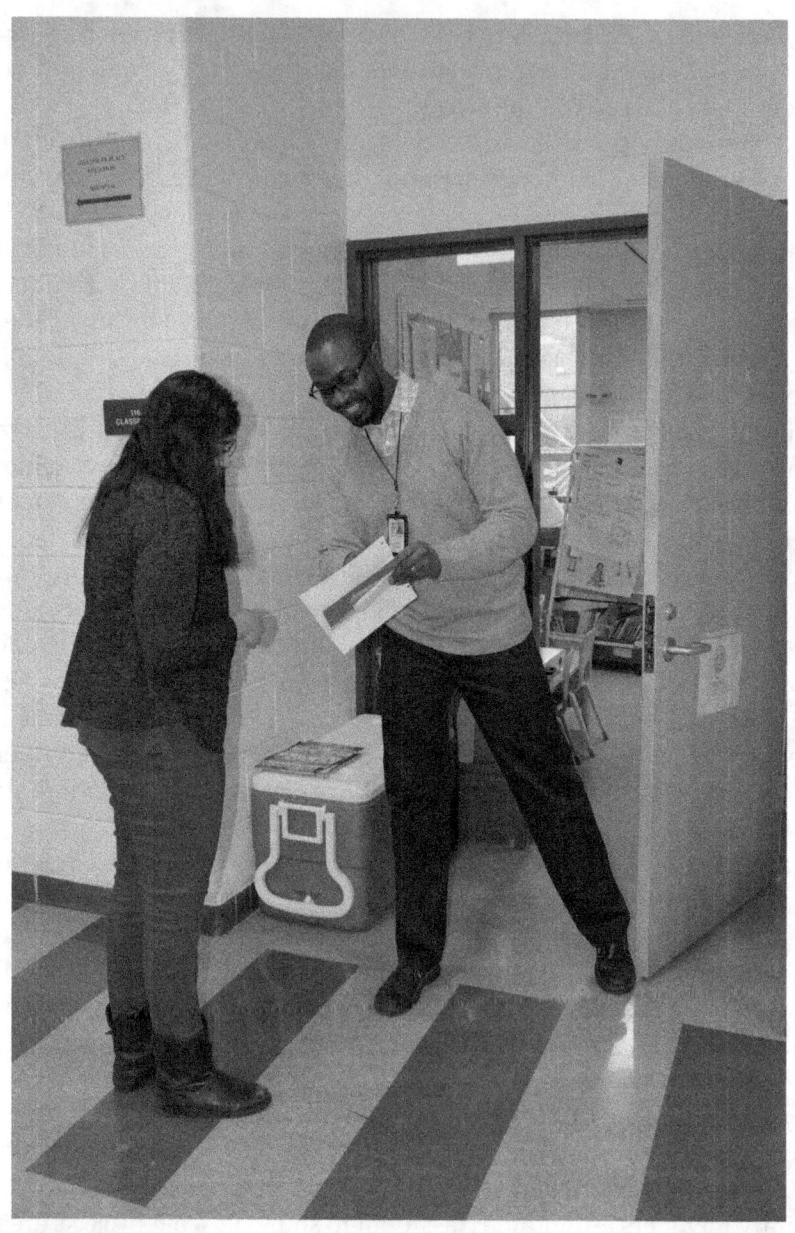

FIGURE 5.5 At pick up, a preschool teacher shares a positive behavior report with a parent.

Although an excellent strategy for communicating brief, positive anecdotes, drop off and pick up time does not generally allow for the dissemination of general classroom information or more complex information about children's behavior, progress, and learning. Notes, either on paper or via e-mail, as well as scheduled conversations, provide opportunities for families and teachers to connect to one another over their shared investment in children's education and development (Wong & Wong, 2004). Blogs and newsletters allow families to gain an understanding of the day-to-day activities and routines in your classroom. Pictures are essential parts of these communications and are effective tools to help convey the day-to-day goings on in your classroom. With the widespread use of technology, you can send text and picture messages via cell phone, websites, or smartphone apps to families if care is taken not to violate the privacy of the children in your classroom. Many schools and centers today use a learning management system such as Blackboard to provide secure communication spaces for family communication. Written and electronic communication provides a great connection to families that you may not otherwise have much contact with—families with nannies or other caregivers, or

FIGURE 5.6 At drop off, a child shows her mother how to use the sparkle paint at a classroom center.

FIGURE 5.7 Cubbies and coat racks inside of the classroom invite parents into your space during drop off and pick up.

those parents who do not ever come to school. An additional advantage of written communication is that it can be translated in many languages either by a native speaker (preferred) or one of the translation resources. An example of a written communication from the teacher to families is shown below.

Hello Purple Families!

We did so much playing outside this week in the beautiful weather. We visited both the park and community garden, and one day we even went to both. Did you hear about our fairy houses and gardens? This was an interest that the kids had in the fall, and we've revived it now that the warm weather is back. We started the week by building fairy houses, gardens, woods, and farms at the playground. . . .

We wanted more materials to build with, so the next day we headed to the community garden to use some big grape vines that were cut down and piled in the back.

We built an amazing house and the kids spent a long time decorating it with bark, creating furniture with stones and sticks, and collecting food for the fairies like berries and leaves. We even found some treasures like a pink gem and some chunks of broken mosaic, and we left them there for the fairies to enjoy. We did lots of speculating about how big fairies are, what they eat, and how you know if they've visited.

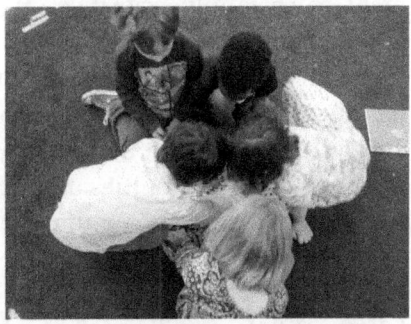

We came back the next day and the house was still there! The kids noticed that some things had been moved around, and they thought maybe fairies really did visit!

On Thursday we headed to the park to play, but we brought some vines with us to build again . . . and to paint! We built a big beautiful house/garden, and painted it with bright colors. It was tricky to paint the branches once they were up—it required lots of fine motor control—but kids worked hard at it.

Next week, in response to popular demand, we will have show and tell! Please have your child bring in an object from home on Wednesday. We request nothing with a violence/fighting theme. We also look forward to having Shenese's cousin, a professional tap dancer, visit us on Tuesday for a dancing demonstration.

Thanks, and have a great weekend!

Once you have welcomed families into their classroom community, taking the time to talk with families about their priorities and needs strengthens home/school relationships. Every family has needs related to their family functions (social-emotional, financial, spiritual, daily care, etc.) (Keilty, 2016) and these needs will change as their situation changes. Perhaps a family is expecting a new baby or has taken over the care of a cousin. Maybe the family will take an extended trip to visit grandparents in Mexico. A family may have difficulty accessing health care to complete their child's vaccines or asthma management. Such family priorities often take precedence over immediate involvement in a child's education. When you take time to ask how the family is doing and connect families to resources when necessary, families then become freed to prioritize educational needs. Teachers are well served to become familiar with community resources—which include faith communities, food pantries, mental health services, and after-school programs—and connect families to resources as needed. In larger cities, there are often programs like asthma vans or mobile dentists that will come to the school and provide services for children for free. All the families need to do to access the services is sign a permission slip and make sure their child is at school the day the asthma van comes.

Problem-solve Together

Once you have established a positive relationship with families, problem solving together will further strengthen that bond. During your conversations with families, check in about whether anything has changed at home, how the child is sleeping, and if similar behaviors are present at home. Often when you listen to families you can get to the root of the behavioral problem rather than reacting and intervening only after the behavior has occurred. Functional behavior assessment (FBA) is an effective framework to follow when collecting data about the ABCs of the behavior: **A**ntecedent, challenging **B**ehavior, and the immediate **C**onsequence. The Antecedent is the event that happens right before the challenging behavior, the Behavior is what the child does that you want to stop them from doing, and the Consequence is what happens immediately after the Behavior. The Consequence portion of the ABC data collection can be tricky. Many of us think of consequences as punishments or something that we decide on. With challenging behaviors, the consequence is what happens immediately following the behavior, not something that happens later as an adult reaction to the behavior. For example, while teaching second grade, I worked with a student, Cyrus, who was usually very engaged and greeted me happily each day. Every day during writer's workshop, he engaged in challenging behaviors including wandering around the room, kicking the bottom rungs of his desk to make a horribly loud noise, throwing/dropping all his materials so that he had to get up and get them, and saying inappropriate things to the children nearby. Each time this happened, I redirected Cyrus or moved him away from his peers. Once, I had to send him to the principal's office (the school's required disciplinary procedure) after he used profanity. By taking notes about the Antecedent (writing workshop started), what the Behavior entailed (getting up, mostly) and the immediate Consequence of the behavior (avoiding writing), Cyrus's mother and I determined that he used these behaviors to escape from a task that was very difficult for him (writing). His mother reported that he enjoyed drawing at home but refused to write words. We decided to allow him to draw illustrations of his ideas first and then, if needed, ask me for help with writing about them. This helped Cyrus to complete the work and feel successful so that he no longer engaged in challenging behaviors during writing time. It also allowed for me to concentrate on the specific skill development he needed assistance with rather than his behaviors. With interventions to help Cyrus develop his writing skills, the behaviors stopped completely by the end of the year. I never heard a profane word out of his mouth again. Cyrus's mother and I met to solve this challenging behavior at a convenient time for both her schedule, which included working for an employer who would dock her for leaving early, and my allowable hours for being on school property. Thus, honoring family schedules is an important aspect of establishing and building relationships with families.

Involve Families in Scheduling Meetings and School Events
When scheduling school events, meetings with families to address challenges, or meetings to create official special education plans, it is imperative to include the family in logistical planning. Many families do not have jobs that easily allow day-time meetings or easily accessible child care. Prior to scheduling the meeting with other school staff, ask the family about days of the week and times that work well for them. One school reported substantial increases in family participation

in monthly curriculum nights after surveying families about what times and days of the week worked best for them (Skiles, Strange, Kuhl, Lubel, & Potts, 2016). For less-formal meetings, consider the available technological resources, including Google Hangouts, Facetime, smartphone apps, or Skype. Although not all families have access to these tools, those who do may be more likely to attend meetings if they can attend remotely during a lunch hour or younger child's nap time. However the communication occurs, it is important that it be regular, so that families with children with challenging behaviors don't feel discouraged.

Report Successes More Often Than Failures and Give It Time

Unfortunately, changing behaviors takes time but humans like immediate gratification. Some interventions, including differential attention (DA) for mildly challenging behaviors (for example, ignoring a tantrum), are often met with a spike in the behavior at the start of the intervention before the behavior stops. When you start to see improvements, focus on reporting small successes to the family. This helps them understand that you see the benefit to the effort everyone is putting forth. Families will become fatigued with constant reports of poor behavior. For example, the first day that we implemented Cyrus's illustration-first plan, he sat without engaging in challenging behaviors for 4 minutes before becoming frustrated and breaking the tips off all his pencils repeatedly so that he had to continuously walk to the pencil sharpener. This wasn't the target behavior of sitting at his desk and working through all 25 minutes of writing workshop, but it was significantly better than he had done previously. I reported to his mother at the end of the day that we saw a mild improvement. Cyrus, his mother, and I felt proud of the progress he made, which in turn motivated all of us to work even harder the next day. Communicating Cyrus's successes in front of Cyrus also helped for him to begin changing his thoughts about himself. Instead of the child who was always in trouble, we taught him that he was capable of meeting behavioral expectations and that we were proud of him. Cyrus built his confidence through his daily successes.

Behavioral change will not happen overnight, even with the best combination of parental involvement and intervention. On average, it takes an adult about 66 days to create a habit or break a negative habit (Lally, van Jaarsveld, Potts, & Wardle, 2010). Once you and the family have agreed on an intervention for a challenging behavior, make sure that you are consistently adhering to that intervention for at least a few weeks before deciding whether the intervention is successful. This data can also help the teacher and family to pinpoint the root cause of the behaviors and implement home and school strategies to stop the behaviors before they start. It can be very helpful to take baseline data about the frequency, duration, and intensity of the behaviors as well as the antecedent and consequences of behaviors prior to the intervention, midway through the intervention, and once the intervention has been in place for a few weeks. This data give concrete examples to families about the success of the intervention. When using DA (deliberate ignoring of undesired but not dangerous behaviors), expect that the behaviors may become heightened initially (Bayat, 2015). The child has become accustomed to a response and will continue to attempt to elicit one from you until it has been made very clear that a response is not forthcoming. In addition to regular and specific communication about routine issues and challenging behavior, you will need to think about ways to handle extreme situational behavior.

Communicating Difficult News or Major Concerns

While I was working in early intervention, I was assigned to work with a toddler named Annabel. Annabel lived with her mother, who was 19, and her grandmother. Annabel's mother, Maya, informed me immediately after we met that she did not believe that Annabel needed any intervention. I was there only because Annabel's grandmother insisted Annabel be evaluated when she failed to meet communication milestones at her 2-year checkup. Maya allowed me into the house, and she never missed an appointment, but only because it was a condition of living rent-free with her mother. "Since you're here," Maya told me, "you may as well teach her something." I got to work building a relationship with Maya and Annabel. I made sure to communicate directly with Maya rather than her mother. Maya began to feel empowered to make decisions about therapy goals and even began to sit with us while Annabel and I worked on communication and other play skills. Although I am not qualified to diagnose children (educators seldom, if ever, should give a diagnosis), I knew with all my heart that Annabel had all the behaviors consistent with a diagnosis of autism. She exhibited all the classic signs—a lack of eye contact and inability to play with toys (she would spin the wheels of her cars in front of her eyes for hours), and she used only a few words (juice, truck, Elmo) consistently.

Based on Maya's initial reaction to Annabel's speech delay, I knew that I had to tread lightly bringing up my concerns about Annabel's development with Maya. I started slowly by asking if Maya always spun the wheels on her trucks instead of playing. Maya noticed that Annabel did that, too. The next week I asked if Annabel made eye contact with her mother or if it was just me that she avoided looking at. Maya confirmed again that Annabel didn't make eye contact. I communicated to Maya that we wanted to keep a watch on this behavior because it could be a red flag. I did not say what the red flag might indicate and Maya did not ask. After about a month of my sharing one or two concerns each week, Maya shared with me her concerns about Annabel's ability to recite whole songs from her favorite show but inability to ask for help. It was then that I communicated my concerns about Annabel's symptoms and spoke with Maya about how many of the symptoms were red flags for autism. Maya became quiet and did not say anything else to me the rest of the session. I let her know that when she was ready, we could use an online screening tool to determine if follow-up was needed. When I came to the home the following week, Maya completed the screening tool herself and the results stated that Annabel was at high risk for autism. I connected Maya and Annabel to a developmental pediatrician that I felt was a good fit for them. We continued therapy for the six months that Annabel had to wait for an appointment and brought in an occupational and speech therapist. Each week, Maya and I discussed the progress Annabel made and strategies to address the challenges she presented. One day, Maya called me to let me know that Annabel had been given an autism diagnosis. When I asked how she felt about the news, Maya replied, "Well, we already pretty much knew. This doesn't change the amazing little person that she is."

It is not uncommon for those of us in early childhood to be the first person to notice developmental challenges that a child may exhibit. We are educated to be experts in development and can pick out the ages of babies in grocery carts and children at the park without even trying. Many families haven't received any training in what to expect from their young children so they do not know what is typical. Without realizing it, families often adjust their home routines to compensate for any quirks or developmental delays a child exhibits. Annabel's mother and grandmother became experts at reading Annabel's cues to determine when she would become hungry or thirsty. They only bought her clothes without tags and presented her with foods that they knew she would eat. Annabel couldn't tolerate the texture of paint, sand, or dirt on her hands, so her mother and grandmother kept these textures away from her to avoid meltdowns. In classrooms, these quirks and delays are more likely to impact functioning because it is harder to accommodate for them within a large group, especially when a child cannot communicate exactly what is upsetting them—but a relationship with a family can reveal some of the triggers for meltdowns. Talking to families about these concerns is a difficult task even for the most seasoned practitioner. Breaking the news of your concerns goes more smoothly when you slowly communicate one concern at a time using specific examples and invite families to communicate their concerns with you, back up your opinion with a screening tool, and have a plan about how to address your concerns.

In the vignette with Maya and Annabel, Maya was not ready to hear my concerns about the possibility that her daughter had autism when we met. In fact, Maya wasn't ready to accept that Maya had developmental delays at that time. Although I immediately had concerns about Annabel, I knew that dropping the word *autism* into a conversation during that first meeting would backfire and would likely alienate Maya. By addressing one concern or behavior at a time, I gave Maya time to process the challenges that Annabel presented while not contradicting all the positive thoughts and feelings that Maya had about Annabel. After all, Annabel was and remains an awesome and lovable little girl. She just happens to be an awesome and lovable little girl with autism. As you identify concerns, slowly communicate them to families. Make sure that you are communicating their child's strengths as well. This helps parents to view their child as a complete person, with emphasis on honoring the child they love so dearly, instead of turning their baby into a laundry list of concerns and challenges. It also communicates to parents that you value their child and are aware of their strengths. Approaching the breaking of difficult news this way helps to build the trust in your relationship with the family.

As you express concerns with families, give very specific examples of concerns. With Maya, I first pointed out I noticed Annabel always played with her trucks by spinning the wheels in front of her eyes. This allowed for Maya to connect the concern that I had to behaviors she may have witnessed at home. This specific example also communicated to Maya that I was getting to know Annabel and that I understood her as a person. As time progressed, Maya could come to me with examples of behaviors as well. Ultimately, collecting these anecdotes about Annabel allowed us to work together to address the challenges in Annabel's behavior and the delays in her development. These anecdotes were invaluable in charting her progress and communicating our concerns to Annabel's developmental pediatrician and other service providers, including speech and occupational therapists.

When Maya was ready, I took advantage of the M-CHAT (Robbins, Fein, & Barton, 1999), an online screening tool for autism in toddlers to provide more concrete information for Maya about Annabel's development. It also served to support my clinical opinion so that the "blame" for the news of Annabel's autism risk was not solely placed on me. Most preschool programs require the use of developmental screening tools, including the Ages and Stages questionnaire or the ESI-R (Meisels, Marsden, Wiske, & Henderson, 2008). Utilizing these tools makes concerns you bring to the family more concrete and helps to target the areas of development that the child will need a referral in.

Once you have slowly communicated your concerns and completed a screening instrument, it is time to sit down with the parents and lay out all your concerns. This should be done in a private meeting, without the child present, if possible, and may include other professionals such as the school speech pathologist and/or social worker. Schedule time for the family to ask questions and process their feelings about the concerns you share. Begin with their child's strengths and be prepared with a referral for early intervention, developmental pediatrician, or other service provider, including speech, occupational, or physical therapists. It is imperative to have a plan as to how you and the school will help support the child and family through the referral and diagnosis process. One of the greatest stressors for families is the unknown (Walsh, 2003). If your school has a social worker or other mental health specialist, it is highly recommended to incorporate these services into the plan. Families with children with developmental delays experience significant emotional responses including denial, grief, anger, or sadness. Connecting families with a healthy outlet for these emotions will benefit the entire family. After Annabel's diagnosis, Maya connected with another young mother at Annabel's preschool who had a child on the autism spectrum. The two formed a deep bond and accessed their friendship to relieve some the stress of mothering young children with autism, process their grief and fears, and celebrate their family successes in a constructive, healthy way.

Once a diagnosis has been made, it is key for you to support families with information about the diagnosis and services available for the child and family. When surveyed, families often cited the need for information and the type of information provided as a key factor in positive perceptions of teachers and other service providers (Cho & Gannoti, 2005; Ziviani, Feeney, & Khan, 2011). This means that you'll need to seek out your own information about disabilities in the form of books, online videos, professional development workshops, and available community resources. Besides facilitating family intervention for children with challenging behavior and special needs, there may be occasions when developing a relationship with families is difficult due to the current level of the family's functioning.

Challenging Families

There are certainly situations occurring in children's lives that make it difficult to create effective school-home partnerships. Many children come from homes in which both parents work long hours. Parents may not be able to take off work during school hours to participate in conferences, school activities, or other events. One school sent a survey home to families to determine why family involvement at their school was so poor. An overwhelming number of families cited both a lack of child care for other children and the inconvenient times of days as the main barriers (Skiles et al., 2016). The school offered child care and immediately saw a 40% increase in family attendance. Once the school scheduled monthly events at varying times and days, administrators found an increase of 17% in family participation. Additionally, families were more likely to support literacy, math, and science at home after attending a school function that created opportunities for make-and-take materials with a model from an educator about how to utilize the materials with the child.

In situations wherein families are struggling with mental health, addiction, poverty, domestic violence, or other challenges, it's likely the family will need assistance meeting their immediate needs for safety, shelter, and food before they can assist with challenging classroom behaviors. These families may appear to be hard to reach, but keep in mind they are likely doing the best they can in their current situation. As stated before, it is very beneficial to be well acquainted with community resources to help meet the basic needs of the children and families served. Although you may feel powerless when working with children who are experiencing such incredible stressors at home, there are actions you can take. First and foremost, you can ensure that the child feels safe and valued in the classroom. You do this by creating predictable routines, providing positive feedback for the child, and allowing the child a safe space to be. When assigning homework, be mindful of the child's home environment and intentionally create activities and assignments that do not penalize children from impoverished homes or those experiencing other crises.

Remember That You and the Family Are on the Same Team

Perhaps the most important strategy to working effectively with families is to remember that schools and families are on the same team, working toward the same goal: helping children to become functional, productive members of society. Often in my career, I have spoken with professionals who forget that we are on the same team as the families of the children whom they are working with. It can be incredibly frustrating to work with a child whose family appears not to be involved in their child's education or who has vastly different values from you. Instead of taking on an "us vs. them" attitude, it is helpful to make a list of the family's strengths and the ways in which they are demonstrating a commitment to their child. The best professional compliment I ever received was, "Wow, you really can find something positive about any family." I'm not sure the commenter meant it as a compliment, but I certainly took it as one. Occasionally, we must dig deep to come up with something positive. This is an excellent time to do a cultural competence self-assessment. It is extremely likely that the seeming lack of family strengths has more to do with a lack of understanding of the family culture or the teacher's own cultural beliefs and biases. Once you acknowledge that a family is doing the best possible, you create more opportunities for successful family/school collaboration.

Chapter 5 Activities

1. In your preschool classroom, you wait until Mother's Day each year to have the children complete booklets about their moms and share the information with the class. The children present their booklets with a plant to their mothers at a Mother's Day luncheon. This year, you are reconsidering this activity because last year, there were several children who were sad that their mothers couldn't come. You and your co-teacher are particularly concerned about three students in your class. Affan has very devout Muslim parents. Every day his father brings him to school while his mother waits in the car with her face veiled. Neither of Affan's parents came to Winter conferences. Another student in your class, Sarah, lives with her father and you have never seen or heard about Sarah's mother. Giana's older sister picks her up every day and the girls walk to their aunt's house because their mother works late. Once you called Giana's mother to bring her extra clothes after an accident and her mother said she couldn't leave work. You and your co-teacher love holidays and have planned a lovely Mother's Day luncheon for the last four years. What kinds of activities could you plan instead of the Mother's Day tea?
2. What your money says about your values. List the last five things that you spent money on (even if they seem inconsequential, like a coffee or filling your gas tank). Review your list critically and determine what those purchases tell you about your culture and who you are. Did you purchase this book? That demonstrates a value on learning and striving to become the best teacher you can possibly be. Did you pay your cable bill on time? That demonstrates access to funds, a responsible nature, and a value on entertainment and participation in popular culture. Perhaps you took your youngest child to the doctor for a well-child visit. That shows you value the health and welfare of your children and that you believe in preventative, western medicine. Did you buy an article of clothing? What color is it? How much of your body does it cover? Does it have a logo on it? What would each of these details teach

you about yourself and your culture? What does wearing this article of clothing communicate to others about your culture?

3. Mara is a 3-year-old in your preschool class. She seemed to love coming to school and regularly follows routines and directions. Now that Mara has adjusted to attending school every day, Mara's mother returned to work after being at home with Mara for the last three years. Recently, Mara has refused to take off her coat, and she lays down on the floor and screams and cries each morning when her mother drops her off. Mara's mother leaves the room, watches Mara in the window, and then returns to the classroom for one more hug and kiss to calm Mara down before leaving for good. To distract Mara from her tantrums, you have asked that Mara's mother not return for the second round of hugs and kisses and instead once Mara begins crying you offer to open the block center (Mara's favorite) even though it is time for breakfast and not free play. Mara's mother is no longer late for work, but Mara continues to throw a tantrum every morning. Mara's mother sent you an e-mail expressing her concerns about this new tantrum behavior and included details about Mara's tantrums at home whenever her parents leave Mara with their familiar and beloved babysitter for their weekly date nights. Mara's mother explained that Mara was so upset last weekend that she and her husband stayed home to comfort Mara instead of going out. Using the ABC method of data collection, determine the Antecedent, Behavior, and immediate Consequences of Mara's tantrums. What interventions could you and Mara's family implement to stop the tantrums?

Appendix

Terms to Know

Academic language: the language children need for school, with particular vocabulary for various subjects

Assessment: a process used to determine the degree to which an individual child possesses a particular attribute

Challenging behavior: a child's outburst and loss of self-control

Classroom management: the establishment of procedures and routines to provide structure throughout the learning environment

Conflict resolution: finding a solution that stems from sharing materials, use of space, need for privacy, and so on

Constructivist approach to teaching and learning: the belief that knowledge and behavior are constructed

Cross-cultural zone: the social space where children and teachers of different cultures meet

Cultural competence: the recognition that all cultures have beliefs and values that govern the ways of behaving in families and community

Developmental appropriate practice: the recognition that children are individuals, each with a unique developmental path

Differentiated instruction: provides implementation of various learning strategies and projects to ensure optimal development for each learner

Discipline: the practice of training children to obey rules and/or a code of conduct

Instructional support: careful crafting of discussions, appropriate and timely feedback, and the effective way that you model and support language development

Family: a group of people (two or more) who have committed to being a family and work together to perform family functions

Family functions: all activities that families engage in on a daily or consistent basis to meet their collective and individual needs

Guidance: guiding children in making decisions and recognizing that children's conflicts and "misbehavior" are important learning opportunities.

Management: organizing the learning and providing for the basic safety of the children

Peer modeling/buddy play: pairing children together to teach them appropriate social behavior

Personal schema: individual's thought process

Positive reinforcement: strengthening a desired behavior with meaningful actions or objects to increase the behavior over time

Project approach: in-depth study of a particular topic, usually undertaken by a whole class working on subtopics in small groups, sometimes by a small group of children within a class, and occasionally by an individual child

Social competence: the ability of young children to get along with others

Social construction of the classroom: the plan for small group and large group interactions among children

Social-emotional development: the acquisition of the emotional and social skills for effective functioning

Social-emotional learning: the ways children acquire knowledge, skills, and attitudes to function effectively

Socio-moral atmosphere: the shared values for appropriate behavior in a class

Traffic flow: the plan for the way children move around the room

Universal design for learning: gives everyone a chance to learn and requires you to first and foremost think about multiple means of representing curriculum and strategies

Study Questions

Chapter 1

1. From what you have read, how could you define the meaning of a challenging behavior?
2. Find a child in your classroom whom you think has a challenging behavior and try to find the best techniques to deal with it.
3. Ask your family, friends, or colleagues about how they define a child with a challenging behavior and what they would do to deal with it.

Chapter 2

1. With the child you've identified as having a challenging behavior, what would be a good strategy in establishing a personal relationship with the child?
2. What are the principles that you practice to ensure your classroom is secure and organized? How do you ensure that your learning environment reflects the cultures of the children you serve?
3. What are some of the things that might "bother" the children in your classroom? Create a class meeting where all students get to share their problems and talk about the things that are bothering them in class. Remember to set the ground rules before starting the meeting.

Chapter 3

1. Describe the types of curricula that an educator could use in an early childhood classroom.
2. Why is it important for teachers to know their students and the cultural background that they come from?
3. As a teacher, which curriculum would you think best fits your class? Based on what you have read, implement the best curriculum that you think best fits your classroom.

Chapter 4

1. What are ways teachers could use to create a positive learning environment?
2. What is the difference between management and discipline?
3. Create an ABC chart for a child you think has a challenging behavior and try to change either the Antecedent or the Consequence to be able to change the challenging Behavior.

Chapter 5

1. Why is it important for teachers and families to maintain a positive interaction?

2. What are some of the Antecedents and Consequences that you might want to change in the Behavior of a child whom you think has a challenging behavior? Create an ABC chart and work with the family to make a plan of action.
3. Why is it important to report success more often than failure? How does this apply to your job?

For Additional Information

Center on Response to Intervention
- www.rti4success.org/
- This organization offers a wide range of tools, papers, webinars on ways to implement response to intervention, including best practices for children who present challenging behavior

Center on the Social Emotional Foundations for Early Learning (CSEFEL)
- http://csefel.vanderbilt.edu/resources/wwb/wwb14.html
- The center offers training modules, family information, videos, and statements on hot topics, such as Time Out.

National Head Start Association
- https://www.nhsa.org/
- This association maintains resources useful to programs and families.

National Center on Intensive Intervention
- www.intensiveintervention.org/
- This center provides tools for intervention, such as data-based individualization (DBI).

Positive Behavioral Intervention and Supports
- www.pbis.org/
- This technical assistance site offers materials to support social, emotional, and academic success for all learners with an emphasis on whole school approach.

Responsive Classroom
- www.responsiveclassroom.org/
- This comprehensive model relates social-emotional learning to curriculum with a focus on K-8. The website offers books, blogs, and papers.

Response to Intervention Network
- www.rtinetwork.org/learn/what/whatisrti
- This network shows how to implement a multitiered approach to serve all children with disabilities, including those who present challenging behavior.

Technical Assistance Center on Social Emotional Intervention for Young Children (TACSEI)
- http://challengingbehavior.fmhi.usf.edu/
- This center developed the Pyramid Model to intervention, featuring strategies from the mildest modifications to high-intensity interventions.

The IRIS Center
- http://iris.peabody.vanderbilt.edu/
- This center offers training modules and papers on a wide range of topics related to managing challenging behavior.

WestEd
- www.wested.org/rd_alert_online/helping-early-childhood-educators-deal-with-challenging-behavior/
- This research center offers publications on challenging behavior, English learners, and other salient topics in early childhood.

Zero to Three
- www.zerotothree.org/early-learning/challenging-behaviors
- This site has videos and information guides to use with families and new teachers.

Additional Online Resources

Online Modified Checklist for Autism in Toddlers (M-CHAT), https://m-chat.org/

Early Intervention is a federally mandated program that provides special education services to young children. Early Intervention requirements, fees, and services vary by state but the initial evaluation is always free of charge. A complete listing of Early Intervention State Offices can be found at www.autismspeaks.org/early-access-care/ei-state-info.

The Illinois Early Intervention Training Program (EITP) provides web-based trainings (many are free!). You can access the trainings anywhere in the United States with an Internet connection, and many of the trainings are online modules that can be completed at any time. Find the EITP online training listing here: https://illinois.edu/blog/view/6039/175193. EITP maintains a list of online training related to early childhood sponsored by other entities here: http://illinoiseitraining.org/page.aspx?module=15.

The Ounce, an organization committed to improving the lives of young children, has a YouTube channel with videos that are helpful to share with families about the importance of early learning: www.youtube.com/user/theounceofprevention.

The Division for Early Childhood (DEC) published guidelines for best practice in working with children with special needs and provided examples of each standard. DEC best practice strongly emphasizes working collaboratively with families and provides examples of how to accomplish their partnerships. The best practice guidelines are helpful in your work with all families, not only families with special needs: https://divisionearlychildhood.egnyte.com/dl/v7NSuEwqYX.

A quick guide to FBA can be found here: www.ideapartnership.org/documents/ASD-Collection/asd-dg_Brief_FBA.pdf

Communities in Schools (CIS) specializes in bringing community resources into schools to meet medical, mental health, educational, recreational, and basic needs including food, shelter, and clothing. There are 161 locations in 25 states across the United States. Learn more here: http://www.communitiesinschools.org/

Google Translate (https://translate.google.com/) offers written translation into 100 different languages.

POSITION STATEMENT

Identification of and Intervention with Challenging Behavior

August 2007

DEC strongly believes that the early identification of children with serious challenging behavior is critical to providing effective interventions that will decrease the likelihood of poor academic and social outcomes.

There is growing evidence that young children who engage in chronic problem behaviors proceed through a predictable course of ever-escalating challenging behaviors. These challenging behaviors can lead to both short- and long-term negative consequences for the child and family. It also has been well documented that social emotional competence during the early childhood years is predictive of positive social and school outcomes in elementary school and beyond. Children who can communicate their needs and emotions in appropriate ways, form relationships with peers and adults, solve social problems, and control their emotions are more likely to be successful in school. There is a critical need to identify children with challenging behavior early in order to increase the likelihood of school success and decrease the trajectory toward more severe social and academic problems.

In order to accurately identify children who exhibit challenging behavior, comprehensive assessment approaches are needed. First, screening and assessment should be conducted in a variety of settings in which young children spend time. Second, assessment approaches should be comprehensive and include observations of children in their natural environments. Third, parents and other family members should be integrally involved in the screening and assessment process. Fourth, a team-based process that includes input from family members and professionals from a variety of disciplines should be used. Finally, assessment approaches that can be used to develop effective interventions should be included and there should be a clear link between assessment information and intervention strategies.

DEC strongly believes that partnerships between families, service providers, and caregivers in which each family's unique strengths, concerns, and responsibilities are fully recognized are critical to the design and implementation of interventions to prevent and remediate challenging behavior and to support appropriate behavior.

Effective partnerships between early educators, families, and other team members can facilitate identification of the variables that trigger and maintain the challenging behavior, followed by development and implementation of interventions that support the use of more appropriate behaviors. Effective partnerships also focus on developing strategies that build on the strengths and effective practices of team members.

DEC acknowledges the central role that families play in evaluating and addressing challenging behavior. Families may be able to share information about strategies that have been tried in the past, how their child's behavior varies across settings, the impact of challenging behavior on the family, family goals for their child's behavior, and they can implement interventions in the home and other community or natural environments. The level and type of family involvement should be determined by the family, based on family priorities, rather than prescribed by professionals or programs.

All decisions regarding the identification and assessment of challenging behavior, potential interventions, and evaluation of the effectiveness of interventions must be made in accordance with the family through the Individualized Education Plan or Individualized Family Service Plan if the child has one; or if not, through some other team decision-making processes.

POSITION STATEMENT: Identification of and Intervention with Challenging Behavior

DEC strongly believes that there are effective intervention approaches that may be used to address challenging behavior and support the development of young children's social emotional competence and communication skills.

The range of interventions and supports that are effective in addressing challenging behavior can be conceptualized using the three-tiered public health model of prevention and intervention approaches. The first tier, universal practices, includes strategies designed to promote the development of communication skills, appropriate behaviors, and social competence in all children. Secondary tier interventions include the targeted instruction of social and emotional skills and effective communication skills for children who are at risk for social emotional delays or the development of challenging behavior.

At the tertiary level, individualized interventions, based on an understanding of the behavior in the context where it occurs, provide an effective approach to addressing concerns about challenging behaviors that are persistently used by a child. A functional assessment process should identify the triggers, maintaining consequences, and functions of the challenging behavior. The intervention plan then must be tailored to fit the unique circumstances of the child and the child's family, and should include strategies for teaching the child new skills in addition to problem behavior reduction and prevention strategies. The intervention plan should be designed for implementation by family members and/or early educators in all relevant environments.

In summary, DEC believes that families and early educators must work together to address challenging behavior. This will involve: a) employing comprehensive assessment approaches that include screening and identification of the triggers, maintaining consequences, and the function of behavior; b) implementing a variety of evidence-based strategies and services designed to prevent challenging behavior, to remediate chronic and intensive challenging behavior, and to teach and support social and emotional competence and appropriate communicative and adaptive behavior; and c) providing support to team members as they develop and implement intervention plans in natural environments.

APPROVED BY THE DEC EXECUTIVE BOARD: APRIL 1998
ENDORSED BY THE NATIONAL ASSOCIATION FOR THE EDUCATION OF YOUNG CHILDREN: 1999
REAFFIRMED: JUNE 5, 2001
ENDORSED BY THE NATIONAL HEAD START ASSOCIATION, NATIONAL CHILD CARE RESOURCE AND REFERRAL ASSOCIATION, NATIONAL BLACK CHILD DEVELOPMENT INSTITUTE AND NATIONAL ASSOCIATION OF BILINGUAL EDUCATORS: 2003
REAFFIRMED: AUGUST 21, 2007
ENDORSED BY THE INFANT TODDLER COORDINATOR ASSOCIATION: 2008

Division for Early Childhood
27 Fort Missoula Road • Missoula, MT • 59804 • Phone: 406-543-0872 • Fax: 406-543-0887
E-mail: dec@dec-sped.org • www.dec-sped.org

Permission to copy not required – distribution encouraged.

Standing Together Against Suspension & Expulsion in Early Childhood

A Joint Statement

Every year, as many as 8,710 3- and 4-year-old children may be expelled from or pushed out of their state-funded preschool or prekindergarten classroom.[i] A disproportionate number of these children are African American boys and girls, and these early childhood expulsions are happening at a rate more than three times that of their older peers in grades K–12.[ii] In child care centers, expulsion rates are 13 times what they are in K–12 classrooms, with as many as 39 percent of child care providers reporting at least one expulsion in the past year.[iii] Many more children, both with and without diagnosed disabilities, across all early childhood settings and sectors, are suspended, with data reflecting severe racial disparities. Indeed, while African American children make up 18 percent of public school preschool enrollment, they represent 48 percent of preschoolers suspended more than once, leaving them with few supports and fewer options to ensure they are able to participate in high-quality early learning during this critical period in their development.[iv]

In December 2014, the US Department of Health and Human Services and the US Department of Education jointly released a policy statement designed to start pushing these numbers and disparities down toward zero.

As some of the leading organizations addressing early childhood education, we stand united in support of the policy statement and its recommendations, believing deeply that it is our collective responsibility to facilitate equitable access to high-quality, developmentally appropriate, and culturally responsive early childhood education that helps families and communities thrive. We must continue to shine a light on data that inform our decision making, while we work together to create systems, policies, and practices that reduce disparities across race and gender, preventing and eventually eliminating expulsions and suspensions in early childhood settings.

These efforts, whether they are focused on establishing clear policies and guidelines; increasing access to early childhood mental health consultation and crisis counseling; diversifying our teacher pipeline; ensuring that all early educators engage in meaningful professional development that supports them in being culturally responsive, cognizant of bias, and focused on relationship development; providing wrap-around services; or investing in meaningful family engagement, require a collaborative and sustained commitment that includes increasing supports and compensation for educators across settings and sectors – and every one of us has a part to play.

To lead the way, we look to the good work happening in states, communities, and classrooms across the country, and to the resources, recommendations, and supports being developed and shared by many of our own organizations.[v]

We know that young children thrive in the context of stable, supportive relationships with adults who love, teach, and care for them. Expulsions and suspensions in early childhood education both threaten the development of these positive relationships and are a result of the lack of positive relationships between educators, families and children. Expelling preschoolers is not an intervention. Rather, it disrupts the learning process, pushing a child out the door of one early care and education program, only for him or her to be enrolled somewhere else, continuing a negative cycle of revolving doors that increases inequality and hides the child and family from access to meaningful supports.

We support all efforts to help our national, state, district, and classroom policies catch up to what we know is right—ensuring that all children have a safe space in which to play, learn, and grow.

This joint statement was drafted by the National Association for the Education of Young Children (NAEYC), with support from the organizations that signed on. For more information, please email advocacy@naeyc.org.

American Academy of Pediatrics
American Federation of Teachers
American Psychological Association
Attendance Works
BUILD Initiative
Children's Defense Fund
Child Care Aware of America
Center for Law and Social Policy
Defending the Early Years
Division for Early Childhood of the Council for Exceptional Children
Early Care and Education Consortium
First Focus
First Five Years Fund
FirstSchool
IDEA Infant Toddler Coordinators Association
MomsRising
National Association for the Education of Young Children
National Association for Elementary School Principals
National Association for Family Child Care
National Association of Early Childhood Specialists in State Departments of Education
National Association of Early Childhood Teacher Educators
National Association of State Directors of Special Education
National Black Child Development Institute
National Council of La Raza
National Education Association
National Head Start Association
National Urban League
National Women's Law Center
Nemours Children's Health System
New America
Ounce of Prevention
Save the Children
Save the Children Action Network
Zero to Three

---

[i] This calculation is based on data indicating that there are 1.3 million children in state-funded pre-K (served in public school, Head Start, and community-based child care settings), according to NIEER's 2014 State of Preschool report, and assuming a rate of expulsion of 6.7 out of 1,000 children in state-funded preK, according to the Gilliam study (Gilliam, W.S., 2005. *Prekindergarteners left behind: Expulsion rates in state prekindergarten systems.* Policy Brief series no. 3. New York, NY: Foundation for Child Development). Although this statement on expulsion and suspension—and much of the related work—has grown in part out of the Office for Civil Rights (OCR) data, we do not cite only the OCR 2011–2012 report for several reasons: (1) OCR itself includes several cautions in analyzing the data due to the non-sampling error in self-reported data; (2) the OCR data are limited to public preschool programs (which may be part of state pre-K programs or may be separate from those programs); and (3) the fact that expulsion in preschool may not follow typical K-12 expulsion procedures and reporting requirements. Teacher surveys, like those used in the Gilliam study, may be a more reliable and accurate way to assess preschool expulsions and "push-outs," versus the Civil Rights Data Collection (CRDC) data, which rely on a school district's report of student counts.
[ii] Gilliam, W. S. (2005). Prekindergarteners left behind: Expulsion rates in state prekindergarten systems. New York, NY: Foundation for Child Development.
[iii] Gilliam, W.S., & Shahar, G. (2006). Preschool and child care expulsion and suspension: Rates and predictors in one state. *Infants & Young Children*, 19, 228–45.
[iv] US Department of Education, Office for Civil Rights (2014). *Data Snapshot: Early Childhood Education Highlights.* Issue Brief #2.
[v] For a partial list of available resources, please see the associated Suspension and Expulsion in Early Childhood Resource Page.

References

Alsaker, F. D., & Gutzwiller-Helfennger, E. (2010). Social behavior and peer relationships of victims, bully-victims, and bullies in kindergarten. In S. R. Jimerson, S. M. Swearer, & D. L. Espelage (Eds.), *Handbook of bullying in schools: An international perspective.* New York: Routledge.

American Montessori Society. (2016). *Montessori Education.* Retrieved from http://amshq.org/

Bailey, D., Hebbeler, K., & Scarborough, A. (2003). *Families' first experiences with early intervention.* Menlo Park, CA: SRI International.

Bailey, R., Jones, S. M., Jacob, R., Madden, N., & Phillips, D. (2012). Social, Emotional, and Cognitive Understanding and Regulation in education (SECURe): Preschool program manual and curricula. Cambridge, MA: Harvard University.

Bayat, M. (2015). *Addressing challenging behaviors and mental health issues in early childhood.* New York: Routledge.

Bender, W. N. (2012). *Project-based learning: Differentiating for the 21st century.* Thousand Oaks, CA: Corwin.

Berry, C. F., & Mindes, G. (1993). *Planning a theme-based curriculum: Goals, themes, activities and planning guides for 4's and 5's with Carla Berry.* Glenview, IL: Good Year Books.

Bilmes, J. (2012). *Beyond behavior management: The six life skills children need* (2nd ed.). St. Paul, MN: Red Leaf Press.

Blackhurst, E., Carnine, D., Cohen, L., Kame'enui, E., Langone, J., Palley, D., & Stewart, R. (Fall 1999). *Research Connections in Special Education: Universal Design N. 5.* Retrieved from http://eric.ed.gov/?id=ED433666

Brady, K., Forton, M. B., Porter, D., & Wood, C. (2003). *Rules in school.* Turner Falls, MA: Northeast Foundation for Children.

Bredekamp, S. (1987). *Developmentally appropriate practice in early childhood programs serving children birth through age 8.* Washington, DC: National Association for the Education of Young Children.

Bronfenbrenner, U. (1986). Ecology of the family as a context for human development: Research perspectives. *Developmental Psychology, 22*(6), 723–742.

Brophy, J., Alleman, J., & Knighton, B. (2010). *A learning community in the primary classroom*. New York: Routledge.

Buggey, T., & Hoomes, G. (2001). Using video self-modeling with preschoolers with autism spectrum disorder: Seeing can be believing. *Young Exceptional Children, 14*(3), 2–12.

Causton, J., & Tracy-Bronson, C. P. (2015). *The educator's handbook for inclusive school practices*. Baltimore, MD: Paul H. Brooks.

Chicago Public Schools. (2016). *CPS Stats and Facts*. Retrieved from http://cps.edu/About_CPS/At-a-glance/Pages/Stats_and_facts.aspx

Cho, S., & Gannotti, M. E. (2005). Korean-American mothers' perception of professional support in early intervention and special education programs. *Journal of Policy and Practice in Intellectual Disabilities, 2*(1), 1–9.

Collaborative for Academic and Social Emotional Learning (CASEL). (2016). *State standards for social emotional learning*. Retrieved from http://www.casel.org/state-standards-for-social-and-emotional-learning/

Cooper, J. E., He, Y., & Levin, B. B. (2011). *Developing critical cultural competence: Guide for 21st century educators*. Thousand Oaks, CA: Corwin.

Copple, C., & Bredekamp, S. (2009). *Developmentally appropriate practice in early childhood programs serving children birth through age 8*. 3rd ed. Washington, DC: National Association for the Education of Young Children.

Crick, N. R., Casas, J. F., & Ku, H-C (1999). Relational and physical forms of peer victimization in preschool. *Developmental Psychology, 35*(2), 376–385.

Curtis, D., & Carter, M. (2015). *Designs for living and learning: Transforming early childhood environments*. 2nd ed. St. Paul, MN: Red Leaf Press.

D'Andrea, K. C. (2015). Children as changemakers: Ecology in action. In Diamond, J., Grob, B., & Reitzes, F. (Eds.), *Teaching kindergarten: Learner-centered classrooms for the 21st century* (pp. 46–55). New York: Teachers College Press.

Davis, K., & Gavidia-Payne, S. (2009). The impact of child, family, and professional support characteristics on the quality of life in families of young children with disabilities. *Journal of Intellectual & Developmental Disability, 34*(2), 153–162.

Delpit, L. (2012). *Multiplication is for white people*. New York: New Press.

Delpit, L. (2013). *Other people's children: Cultural conflict in the classroom.* New York: The New Press.

Derman-Sparks, L., & Edwards, J. O. (2010). *Anti-bias education for young children and ourselves.* Washington, DC: National Association for the Education of Young Children.

Derman-Sparks, L. O., Ramsey, P., & Edwards, J. O. (2011). *What if all the kids are white?* 2nd ed. New York: Teachers College Press.

DeVries, R., & Zan, B. (2012). *Moral classroom, moral children: Creating a constructivist atmosphere in early education.* New York: Teachers College Press.

DeVries, R., Zan, B., Hildebrandt, C., Edmiaston, R., & Sales, C. (2002). *Developing constructivist early childhood curriculum: Practical principles and activities.* New York: Teachers College Press.

Durkheim, E. (1973). *Moral education: A study in the theory and application of the sociology of education.* Translated by Everett K. Wilson & Herman Schnurer. New York: Free Press.

Early Childhood Learning and Knowledge Center [ECLKC] Head Start (2015). *Head Start early Learning outcomes framework.* Retrieved from https://eclkc.ohs.acf.hhs.gov/hslc/hs/sr/approach/elof

Edutopia George Lucas Foundation. (2016). Retrieved from www.edutopia.org/

Edwards, C. P., Gandini, C., & Forman, G. E., (Eds.) (2012). *The hundred languages of children,* 3rd ed. Santa Barbara, CA: Praeger.

Elias, M. J., Zins, J. E., Weissberg, K. S., Frey, M. T., Greenberg, N. M., Kessler, R., Schwab-Stone, M. E., & Shriver, T. P. (1997). *Promoting social and emotional learning: Guidelines for educators.* Alexandria, VA: Association for Supervision and Curriculum Development.

Ensher, G. L., & Clark, D. A. (2011). *Relationship-centered practices in early childhood: Working with families, infants & young children at risk.* Baltimore, MD: Paul H. Brookes.

Epstein, A. S. (2009). *Me, you, us: Social-emotional learning in preschool.* Ypsilanti, MI: High Scope Research Foundation.

Erikson, E. H. (1963). *Childhood and Society.* New York: W.W. Norton & Co.

Essa, E. L., Taylor, J. M., Pratt, J. M., and Roberts, S. A. (2012). The inside-out project: Illustrating the complexity of relationships in kindergarten and first grade. *Young Children, 67*(5), 24–33.

Evans, B. (2002). *You can't come to my birthday party! Conflict resolution with young children.* Ypsilanti, MI: High Scope.

Favazza, P. C., Ostrosky, M. M., & Mouzourou, C. (2016). *The making friends program: Supporting acceptance in your K-2 classroom*. Baltimore, MD: Paul H. Brooks.

Fiedler, C.R., Simpson, R. L., & Clark, D. M. (2007). *Parents and families of children with disabilities: Effective school-based support services*. Englewood Cliffs, NJ: Pearson.

Fox, L., & Lentini, R. H. (2006). You got it! Teaching social and emotional skills. *Young Children, 60*(6), 36–42.

Fromberg, D. F. (2012). *The all-day kindergarten and pre-K curriculum: A dynamic themes approach*. New York: Routledge.

Galindo, C., & Sheldon, S. B. (2012). School and home connections and children's kindergarten achievement gains: The mediating role of family involvement. *Early Childhood Research Quarterly, 27*, 90–103.

Gallagher, K. C. (2013). Guiding children's friendship development. *Young Children, 68*(5), 26–32.

Gallavan, N. P. (2010). *Navigating cultural competence in grades K–5: A compass for teachers*. Thousand Oaks, CA: Corwin.

Gartrell, D. (2004). *The power of guidance: Teaching social-emotional skills in early childhood classrooms*. Clifton Park, NJ: Delmar Learning, a Division of Thomson Learning.

Gilliam, W. S. (2008). Implementing policies to reduce likelihood of preschool expulsion. FCD Policy Brief No. 7. New York: Foundation for Child Development.

Gladden, R. M., Vivolo-Kantor, A. M., Hamburger, M. E., & Lumpkin, C. D. (2014). *Bullying surveillance among youths: Uniform definitions for public health and recommended data elements, version 1.0*. Atlanta, GA: National Center for Injury Prevention and Control, Centers for Disease Control and Prevention and U.S. Department of Education.

Gonzalez-Mena, J. (2014). *50 Strategies for communicating and working with diverse families*. Upper Saddle River, NJ: Pearson.

Good, T. L. & Good, J. (2008) *Looking in classrooms*. 10th ed. Englewood Cliffs, NJ: Pearson.

Gottlieb, M., & Ernst-Slavit, G. (2014). *Academic language in diverse classrooms: Definitions and contexts*. Thousand Oaks, CA: Corwin.

Gray, C. (1996). Teaching children with autism to "read" social situations. In K. Quill (Ed.), *Teaching students with autism: Methods to enhance learning, communication, and socialization* (pp. 219–242). New York: Delmar Publishers.

Gray, C. (2010). *The new social story book: Over 150 social stories that teach every day social skills to children with autism or Asperger's syndrome and *their peers*, revised and expanded 10th anniversary edition. Arlington, TX: Future Horizons.

Green, C. L., Walker, J. M., Hoover-Dempsey, K. V., & Sandler, H. M. (2007). Parents' motivations for involvement in their children's education: An empirical test of the theoretical model of parental involvement. *Journal of Educational Psychology, 99*(3) 532–544.

Gullo, D. F. (2005). *Understanding assessment and evaluation in early childhood education.* New York: Teachers College Press.

Gutzwiller-Helfenfinger, E., Gasser, E., & Malti, T. (2010). Moral emotions and moral judgments in children's narratives: Comparing real-life and hypothetical transgressions. *New Directions in Child and Adolescent Development,* Fall 2010(129), 11–31.

Hancock, C. L., & Carter, D. R. (2016). Building environments that encourage positive behavior: The preschool behavior support self-assessment. *Young Children, 71*(1), 66–73.

Hargreaves, A. (1998). The emotional practice of teaching. *Teaching and Teacher Education, 14*(8), 835–854.

Helm, J. H., & Katz, L. G. (2010). *Young investigators: The project approach in the early years.* New York: Teachers College Press.

Hemmeter, M. L., Fox, L., & Snyder, P. (2013). A tiered model for promoting social-emotional competence and addressing challenging behavior. In Buysse, V. & Peisner-Feinberg, E. S. (Eds.), *Handbook of responsive intervention in early childhood.* Baltimore, MD: Paul H. Brookes.

High Scope Curriculum https://highscope.org/curriculum

Howell, J., & Reinhard, K. (2015). *Rituals and traditions.* Washington, DC: National Association for the Education of Young Children.

Hughes, J. and Kwok, O. (2007). Influence of student–teacher and parent–teacher relationships on lower achieving readers' engagement and achievement in the primary grades. *Journal of Educational Psychology, 99*(1): 39–51.

Hurtubise, K., & Carpenter, C. (2011). Parents' experiences in role negotiation within an infant services program. *Infants and Young Children, 24*(1), 75–86.

IRIS Center at Vanderbilt University. (2016). Module on functional behavior assessment. http://iris.peabody.vanderbilt.edu/module/fba/

Jackson, P. W. (1968). *Life in classrooms.* New York: Holt, Rinehart, and Winston, Inc.

Jones, E. (2012). The emergence of emergent curriculum. *Young Children, 67*(2): 66–68.

Jones, E., & Reynolds, G. (2013). *The play's the thing: The teacher's role in children's play*. 2nd ed. New York: Teachers College Press.

Jones, S. M., Bouffard, S. M., & Weissbourd, R. (2013). Educators' social and emotional skills vital to learning. *Phi Delta Kappan, 94*(8), 62–65.

Joseph, G. E., & Strain, P. S. (2010). Teaching young children interpersonal problem-solving skills. *Young Exceptional Children, 13*(3), 28–40.

Katz, L. G., Chard, S. C., Kogan, V. (2014). *Engaging children's minds: The Project Approach,* 3rd ed. New York: Praeger.

Kaufman, C. (2010). *Executive function in the classroom: Practical strategies for improving performance and enhancing skills for all students.* Baltimore, MD: Paul Brookes.

Keilty, B. (2016). *The early intervention guidebook for families and professionals: Parenting for success* (2nd ed.). New York: Teachers College Press.

Kostelnik, M. J., Soderman, A. K., Whiren, A. P., & Rupiper, M. Q. (2015). *Developmentally appropriate curriculum: Best practices in early childhood education.* 6th ed. Englewood Cliffs, NJ: Pearson.

Kreidler, W. J. (1994). *Teaching conflict resolution through children's literature.* New York: Scholastic Professional Books.

Kreite, R., & Davis, C. (2014). *The morning meeting book K–8*. 3rd ed. Turner Falls, MA: Center for Responsive Schools, Inc.

Ladson-Billings, G. (1992). Culturally relevant teaching: The key to making multicultural education work. In Grant, C. A. (Ed.), *Research and multicultural education* (pp. 106–121). London: Falmer Press.

Ladson-Billings, G. (1994). *The dreamkeepers: Successful teaching for African American students.* San Francisco: Jossey-Bass, pp. 17–18.

Ladson-Billings, G. (1995). Toward a theory of culturally relevant pedagogy. *American Educational Research Journal, 32*(3), 465–491.

Ladson-Billings, G. (2009). *The dreamkeepers: Successful teachers of African American Children.* 2nd ed. San Francisco: Jossey-Bass.

Lally, P., van Jaarsveld, C. H. M., Potts, H.W.W., & Wardle, J. (2010). How are habits formed: Modelling habit formation in the real world. *European Journal of Social Psychology, 40,* 998–1009.

Lamm, S., Groulx, J. S., Hansen, C., Patton, M. M., & Slaton, A. J. (2006). Creating environments for peaceful problem solving. *Young Children, 61*(6), 22–28.

Lavigne, A. L., & Good, T. L. (2013). *Teacher and student evaluation: Moving beyond the failure of school reform.* New York: Routledge.

Levine, E., & Tamburrino, M. (2014). Bullying among young children: Strategies for prevention. *Early Childhood Education Journal, 42*(4), 271–278.

Lickey, D. C., & Powers, D. J. (2011). *Starting with their strengths: Using the project approach in early childhood special education.* New York: Teachers College Press.

Lynch, E. W. (2011). Conceptual Framework: From culture shock to cultural learning. In Lynch, E. W. & Hanson, M. C. (Eds.), *Developing cross-cultural competence: A guide for working with children and their families.* Baltimore, MD: Paul H. Brookes Publishing Co.

Manaster, H. & Jobe, M. (2012). Supporting preschoolers' positive peer relationships. *Young Children, 67*(5), 12–17.

Mayer, J. D., & Salovey, P. (1997). What is emotional intelligence? In P. Salovey & D. J. Sluyter (Eds.), *Emotional development and emotional intelligence: Educational implications* (pp. 3–34). New York: Harper Collins.

McCarthy, C. J., Lineback, S., & Reiser, J. (2014). Teacher stress, emotion, and classroom management. In Emmer, E. T. & Sabornie, E. J. (Eds.), *Handbook of classroom management* (2nd ed., pp. 301–321). New York: Routledge.

McCollum, J. (2015). From qualities of interaction to intervention practices: Using what comes naturally. In *DEC Recommended Practices: Enhancing Services for Young Children with Disabilities and Their Families* (pp. 87–97). Los Angeles, CA: The Division for Early Childhood.

McWilliam, R. A. (2010). *Working with families of young children with special needs.* New York: Guilford Publications.

Meadan, H., Ayvazo, S., & Ostrosky, M. M. (2016). The ABCs of challenging behavior: Understanding basic concepts. *Young Exceptional Children, 19*(1), 3–15.

Meadan, H., Ostosky, M. M., Santos, R. M., & Snodgrass, M. R. (2013). How can I help? Prompting procedures to support children's learning. *Young Exceptional Children, 16*(4), 31–39.

Meier, D., Knoester, M., & D'Andrea, K. C. (Eds.) (2015). *Teaching in themes: An approach to schoolwide learning, creating community and differentiating instruction.* New York: Teachers College Press.

Meisels, S. J., Marsden, D. B., Wiske, M. S., & Henderson, L. W. (2008). *Early screening inventory-revised.* New York: Pearson.

NAEYC. (2009). NAEYC position statement on developmentally appropriate practice in early childhood programs serving children from birth through age 8. Washington, DC: Author.

National Center on Cultural Competence. (2007). *A guide for advancing family-centered and culturally and linguistically competent care.* Washington, DC: Georgetown University.

National Center on Universal Design for Learning. (2016). *What Is Universal Design?* Retrieved from www.udlcenter.org/aboutudl/whatisudl

Neimark, A. (2015). The chairs are theirs: Conflict resolution in a kindergarten classroom. In Diamond, J., Grob, B., & Reitzes, F. (Eds.), *Teaching kindergarten: Learner-centered classrooms for the 21st century* (pp. 108–115). New York: Teachers College Press.

Nemeth, K., & Brilliante, P. (2011). Solving the puzzle: Dual language learners with challenging behaviors. *Young Children, 66*(4), 12–17.

Olweus, D. (2001). Bullying at school: Tackling the problem. *The OECD Observer, 225* (March): 24–26.

Pianta, R. C., La Paro, K. M., & Hamre, B. K. (2008). *Classroom assessment scoring system™ Manual Pre-K.* Baltimore, MD: Paul H. Brookes.

Posten, D. J., Turnbull, A., Park, J., Mannan, H., Marquis, J., & Wang, M. (2003). Family quality of life: A qualitative inquiry. *Mental Retardation, 41*(5), 313–328.

Rapp, W. H. (2015). *Universal design for learning in action: 100 ways to teach all.* Baltimore, MD: Paul H. Brookes Publishing.

Raver, C. C., Blair, C., & Li-Grining, C. (2012). Chapter 5 Extending models of self-regulation to classroom settings: Implications for professional development. In Howes, C., Hamare, B. K., & Pianta, R. C. (Eds.), *Effective early childhood professional development: Improving teacher practice and child outcomes* (pp. 113–130). Baltimore: Paul H. Brookes Publishing.

Richman, K. (2011). Teaching thematically in a standards context. In Sleeter, C. E. & Cornbleth, C. (Eds.), *Teaching with vision: Culturally responsive teaching in standards-based classrooms* (pp. 61–72). New York: Teachers College Press.

Robins, D. L., Fein, D., & Barton, M. L. (1999). Follow-up interview for the modified checklist for autism in toddlers (M-CHAT FUI). Self-published.

Roth, D., & Dinnerstein, R. (2015). In Diamond, J., Grob, B., & Reitzes, F. (Eds.), Saim's wheelchair: Making a transportation study meaningful,

Teaching kindergarten: Learner-centered classrooms for the 21st century (pp. 56–68). New York: Teachers College Press.

Saifer, S., Edwards, K., Ellis, D., Ko, L., & Stucynski, A. (2011). *Culturally responsive standards-based teaching: Classroom to community and back.* 2nd Ed., Thousand Oaks, CA: Corwin.

Schwartz, I., & Woods, J. (2015). Making the most of learning opportunities. In *DEC Recommended Practices: Enhancing Services for Young Children with Disabilities and Their Families.* Los Angeles, CA: Authors.

Serpell, Z. N., & Mashburn, A. J. (2012). Family-school connectedness and children's early social development. *Social Development, 21,* 21–46.

Sheridan, S. M., Bovaird, J. A., Glover, T. A., Garbacz, S. A., Witte, A., & Kwon, K. (2012). A randomized trial examining the effects of conjoint behavioral consultation and the mediating role of the parent teacher relationship. *School Psychology Review, 41,* 23–46.

Skiles, K., Strange, L., Kuhl, L., Lubel, P., & Potts, T. (2016). *Family Involvement: Families and Educators Collaborating to Develop the Whole Child.* Presented at the meeting for the Division of Early Childhood in Louisville, KY.

Stacey, S. (2008). *Emergent curriculum in early childhood settings: From theory to practice.* St. Paul, MN: Red Leaf Press.

Stormont, M., Lewis, T. J., Beckner, R., & Johnson, N. W. (2008). *Implementing positive behavior support systems in early childhood and elementary settings.* Thousand Oaks, CA: Corwin Press.

Sullivan, K. (2011). *The anti-bullying handbook,* 2nd ed. Thousand Oaks, CA: Sage Publishing.

Turnbull, A., Turnbull, R., Erwin, E. J., Soodak, L. C., & Shogren, K. A. (2015). *Families, professionals and exceptionality: Positive outcomes through partnerships and trust* (7th ed.). Upper Saddle River, NJ: Pearson.

US Census Bureau. (2010). Data tools. Retrieved from https://www.census.gov/data.html

US Department of Health and Human Services, Health Resources and Services Administration, Maternal and Child Health Bureau, Division of Services for Children with Special Needs. (2005). *Definition of family-centered care and principles of family-centered care for children.* Rockville, MD: US Department of Health and Human Services.

Vance, E., & Weaver, P. J. (2002). *Class meetings: Young children solving problems together.* Washington, DC: National Association for the Education of Young Children.

Virginia Department of Behavioral Health and Developmental Services. (n.d). *Interpreter Evaluation Form*. Richmond VA: Author.

Walsh, F. (2003). Family resilience: A framework for clinical practice. *Family Process, 42*(1), 1–18.

Wiggins, G., & McTighe, J. (2012). *Understanding by design*, 2nd ed. Alexandria, VA: ASCD.

Williams, J. (2015). Struggle for justice: US history through the eyes of African Americans. In Meier, D., Knoester, M., D'Andrea, K. C. (Eds.), *Teaching in themes: An Approach to Schoolwide Learning, Creating Community, and Differentiating Instruction* (pp. 61–68). New York: Teachers College Press.

Williford, A. P., LoCasale-Crouch, J., Whittaker, J. V., DeCoster, J., Hartz, K. A., Carter, L. M., Wolcott, C. S., & Hatfield, B. E. (2016). Changing teacher-child dyadic interactions to improve preschool children's externalizing behaviors. *Child Development 87*(6), 1–10.

Wong, H. K., & Wong, R. T. (2004). *The first days of school*. Mountain View, CA: Harry K. Wong Publications, Inc.

Wubbolding, R. E. (2011). *Reality therapy*. Washington, DC: American Psychological Association.

Ziviani, J., Feeney, R. B., & Khan, A. (2011). Early intervention services for children with physical disability: Parents' perceptions of family-centeredness and service satisfaction. *Infants and Young Children, 24*(4), 364–382.